Cecilia E. Ford explores the question: what work do adverbial clauses do in conversational interaction? Her analysis of this predominating conjunction strategy in English conversation is based on the assumption that grammars reflect recurrent patterns of situated language use, and that a primary site for language is in spontaneous talk. She considers the interactional, as well as the informational, work of talk, and shows how conversationalists use grammar to coordinate their joint language production. The management of the complexities of the sequential development of a conversation, and the social roles of conversational participants, have been extensively examined within the sociological approach of conversation analysis. Dr. Ford uses conversation analysis as a framework for the interpretation of intercausal relations in her database of American English conversations. Her book contributes to a growing body of research on grammar in discourse, which has until recently remained largely focused on monologic rather than dialogic functions of language.

Studies in Interactional Sociolinguistics 9

General Editor: John J. Gumperz

Grammar in interaction

Studies in Interactional Sociolinguistics

Discourse strategies John J. Gumperz
Language and social identity edited by John J. Gumperz
The social construction of literacy edited by Jenny Cook-Gumperz
Politeness: some universals in language usage Penelope Brown and Stephen C. Levinson
Discourse markers Deborah Schiffrin
Talking voices Deborah Tannen
Conducting interaction Adam Kendon
Talk at work edited by Paul Drew and John Heritage
Grammar in interaction Cecilia E. Ford

Grammar in interaction

Adverbial clauses in American English conversations

CECILIA E. FORD

*Department of English,
University of Wisconsin-Madison*

Published by the Press Syndicate of the University of Cambridge
The Pitt Building, Trumpington Street, Cambridge CB2 1RP
40 West 20th Street, New York, NY 10011-4211, USA
10 Stamford Road, Oakleigh, Victoria 3166, Australia

© Cambridge University Press 1993

First published 1993

Printed in Great Britain at the University Press, Cambridge

A catalogue record for this book is available from the British Library

Library of Congress cataloguing in publication data

Ford, Cecilia E.
    Grammar in interaction: adverbial clauses in American English conversations / Cecilia E. Ford.
        p.   cm. – (Studies in interactional sociolinguistics)
    Includes bibliographical references.
    ISBN 0 521 41803 8 (hardback)
    1. English language – United States – Adverbials. 2. English language – Spoken English – United States. 3. English language – Social aspects – United States. 4. English language – United States – Clauses. 5. Americanisms. 6. Conversation. I. Title.
II. Series.
PE2821.F67 1993
425'0973–dc20   92-8274   CIP

ISBN 0 521 41803 8 hardback

For Dana, Maia, and Sarah

Contents

List of illustrations	*page*	xiii
List of tables		xiv
Acknowledgements		xv
Transcription conventions		xvi
1 Introduction		1
2 Overview of the conversational corpus		21
3 Initial adverbial clauses		26
4 Final versus initial adverbial clauses in continuous intonation		63
5 Final adverbial clauses after ending intonation		102
6 Comparison of clause types and apparent deviations from the general patterns		131
7 Conclusion		146
Notes		151
References		155
Author index		161
Subject index		163

Illustrations

		page
1	Distribution of temporal clauses	132
2	Distribution of conditional clauses	133
3	Distribution of causal clauses	134

Tables

1	Distribution of adverbial clauses by position and type	24
2	Final adverbial clauses by intonation and type	25
3	Initial adverbial clauses	27
4	Types of initial adverbial clauses	62
5	Final adverbial clauses	64
6	Intonation preceding final adverbial clauses	64
7	Adverbial clauses by position and intonation	64
8	Temporal and conditional clauses by primary speakership versus turn-by-turn talk	82
9	Average word length of clauses	89
10	Intonation of final temporal and conditional clauses versus final causal clauses	91
11	Pauses and disfluencies in final temporals and conditionals versus causals	92
12	Final causal clauses after continuing intonation	99
13	Final adverbial clauses added to possibly complete utterances	103
14	Types of post-completion extensions	122
15	Adverbial clause extensions to other speakers' turns	

Acknowledgements

This project was inspired and supported by many friends and teachers, though no one but myself is responsible for the final form it has taken. Jacqueline Lindenfeld originally sparked my interest in language in interaction. Marianne Celce-Murcia pointed me in the direction of adverbial clauses in discourse, and then served as a steady source of feedback and encouragement. Evelyn Hatch has influenced me through her responses to my work and through her dedication to applied linguistics. I thank Barbara Fox for cutting a path between linguistics and conversation analysis in her work on anaphora in English conversation. The work of Deborah Schiffrin has also provided me with a model. I thank her as well for insightful comments on an earlier version of this book. I also thank George Yule for valuable comments and encouragement. The members of a conversation analysis seminar at UCLA in 1986 were generous with their interactional data. In particular, I thank Heidi Riggenbach, Ann Lazaraton, and Betsy Weber.

Two of my teachers deserve special mention. Manny Schegloff has helped me learn the challenges and rewards of looking closely at interaction. And my very special gratitude goes to Sandy Thompson. I cannot capture in words here all that it has meant to me to have had the privilege of working with Sandy.

Work toward the final version of this book was supported by a grant from the Graduate School of the University of Wisconsin-Madison.

Transcription conventions

Symbol	Interpretation
(.)	A short beat of silence
(0.3)	A timed pause
(she)	Parentheses indicate uncertainty about talk
(R):	Uncertainty of identity of speaker
(h)	Breathiness in a word
.hh	Inhalation
hh	Exhalation
thi-	Hyphen indicates a sound cut off in delivery
[	Brackets indicate the onset of simultaneous talk
=	Indicates:

(a) that two utterances are latched to one another without a beat of silence between

e.g., C: Oh::.=
V: =So it's straight...

(b) when parts of a continuous utterance must be transcribed separately

e.g., V: ⌈he's in so much pain, that it seems=
C: ⌊Oh yeah.
V: =like he's never gonna walk again.

she	Underlining indicates stress
SHE	Capitalization of whole words or syllables indicates greater volume than surrounding talk
°she	Indicates lower volume than surrounding talk
she:	Colon indicates elongation of a sound
.	Period indicates ending intonation
,	Comma indicates continuing or "more-to-come" intonation

Transcription conventions

?   Question mark indicates rising intonation

When intervening talk is removed for simplification, this is either stated explicitly or indicated by a series of vertical dots.

1

Introduction

While our understanding of English grammar at the single sentence level is substantial, we are only just beginning to seriously explore patterns of interclausal relations as they are used in naturally occurring language. Furthermore, even though interactional language use outweighs all other types of language use, the analysis of English discourse within linguistics has tended to concentrate on monologue data and to neglect conversation. One reason for this neglect has to do with the relatively recent development of practical and unobtrusive audio and video recording technology. If we hope to gain an understanding of how grammar emerges and changes with use (i.e., an understanding of grammar as a system adapted to its use [Du Bois 1984]), we must make use of the available technology and look more seriously at language in interaction. The present book is a contribution to our understanding of the use of a clause type that is very common in spoken English interaction: the adverbial clause. I examine the use of adverbial clauses in a corpus of naturally occurring American English conversation.

At a general level, this research is part of a larger program of interest in observing grammar in its "natural habitat": connected, contextualized discourse. The focus here is on adverbial clause usage, in part because numerous studies have detailed their functions in discourse and in part because of their relative frequency in spoken English. In addition to contributing to our understanding of adverbial clauses in interactional language use, this study has been guided by a methodological goal: The research presented in this book demonstrates the usefulness of conversation analysis as a tool for understanding the emergence of grammar in interaction.

While the findings reported in this book are compatible with, and informed by, approaches to conversation emerging from speech act theory (for example, Brown and Levinson 1987) as well as those originating in the insights of Goffman (for example, 1967), it is the ethnomethodological variety of conversation analysis which has been central to the work I present here. This chapter, therefore, begins with an introduction to conversation analysis and its value as a way of interpreting talk in interaction, and moves on to a review of adverbial clause usage in English discourse. Through that review, it will become evident that adverbial clauses are of special interest because of their particular functions in discourse.

1.1 Conversation analysis

It is not the case that any study which has as its data talk in interaction is, by nature of such a database, an example of conversation analysis as the term will be used here. Conversation analysis (CA) designates a specific approach to the interpretation of talk in interaction. This approach uses particular methods to discover patterns and substantiate claims about practices of speaking. CA studies present findings and predictions regarding conversation: the structures, mechanisms, and tendencies that operate again and again as interactants share in initiating, maintaining, and closing conversations (for reviews of CA, see Heritage 1984, and Taylor and Cameron 1987).

CA is a relatively autonomous field of research, originating in the work of Sacks, Schegloff and Jefferson (Sacks 1972, 1974; Sacks, Schegloff and Jefferson 1974; Schegloff 1968, 1972, 1976; Jefferson 1973, 1974, 1978). Over the past two decades, an empirical methodology and a large body of findings have developed to investigate the structure of conversational interaction. In relation to various other approaches to the work of talk, CA is unique in being based strictly on naturally occurring data, and in having as its goal accounting for the participants' system for language use in interaction. Making use of audio and video recordings of ordinary interaction, conversation analysts have convincingly demonstrated that the work performed by a piece of talk is inextricably tied to the location of that piece of talk in an inter-

Introduction

actional sequence. They have developed a methodology which relies on a faithfulness to the way that interactants themselves display interpretations of talk. Scholars in the field of CA maintain that an analyst can only arrive at an authentic interpretation when s/he strives to use the talk of the participants themselves as evidence for that interpretation. Working within this framework, researchers have collected conversational data displaying recurrent interactional structures. The CA approach recommends itself to the discourse oriented linguist, both in its empirical methodology and in the extensive body of findngs with which it is associated.[1]

As background for the explication of adverbial clause usage in the present corpus, let me review some basic principles and findings from CA.

1.1.1 *The turn-taking system*

CA offers a set of principles that account for the smooth transfer of speakership across parties in interaction. An understanding of the turn-taking system is essential for a thorough account of the significance of initial versus final placement of adverbial clauses in certain conversational contexts.

It may be so obvious as to seem self-evident that in conversations most commonly one speaker talks at any given time. However, it becomes an intricate task to describe how this minimum of overlapping talk is achieved by conversationalists. Such facts as the following must be accounted for:

> Occurrences of more than one speaker at a time are common, but brief... Transitions (from one turn to a next) with no gap and no overlap are common. Together with transitions characterized by slight gap or slight overlap, they make up the vast majority of transitions...
> (Sacks, Schegloff and Jefferson 1974, pp. 700–701)

One explanation of how interactants are able to so precisely begin their turns relative to the completion of a prior turn lies in the notion of projectability. Turns at talk offer clues as to when they may possibly be complete. So, while one word may be sufficient to do the work of a turn (*Yeah, Who?*), one word may also project that a certain job is to be done in the rest of a turn, and that the turn will not be finished till that work has been done. If a turn is begun with *Is...*, an interactant will probably be correct in assuming that the turn will be a question. As more of the turn is produced, more clues are provided. Through a constellation of grammatical, pragmatic, and intonational signals, turn-completion points can be fairly accurately predicted (Orestrom 1983). In fact, points of overlap can often be understood with reference to notions of projectability and possible completion (Ford and Thompson forthcoming). In example (1), H begins her turn at a point of possible completion in D's turn. D turns out to have one more grammatical unit to add to his turn, but H's prediction of completion is well-founded given the grammatical and intonational signals in D's turn. There is clear falling intonation on *amoebas*.

(1)
    D: Yeah. I mean even they just li:ve with giardia
         an' they li:ve with amoebas. ⌈you know.
    H: ⌊Yeah.   (AM 234)

It is important to note that the mechanics of projectability involves work on the part of the speaker as well as the listener. How turns are transferred is not accounted for merely by the notion of projectability as perceived by listeners; speakers are involved in working out smooth turn transitions as well. The fact that turns are transferred with minimal gaps between them means that the speaker of each turn must be operating under some constraints and must make good on projections by not talking past projected points of completion. Thus, the speaker of a turn is also oriented toward the turn-transfer at points of possible completion.

If a speaker wants an extended turn at talk, there are at least two options. The speaker can avoid interim points of completion within the full length of talk s/he hopes to achieve, points which the interlocutors might (even with all the best, non-interruptive intentions) act upon. Such avoidance of points of possible completion can be achieved through grammar and intonation. As an alternative to avoiding points of possible completion, the speaker can make a special arrangement that will modify the effects of the completion signals s/he may be giving through grammar and intonation. A common modification of the turn-taking system occurs when a story is projected, for example, "A funny thing happened to me..."

In their extensive work with conversational data, Sacks *et al.* (1974) found it useful to develop a vocabulary for referring to the projectable places at which turn-transfer operates. These locations are called *transition-relevance places*. Transition-relevance places are generally located at the ends of *turn-constructional units*, "unit-types with which a speaker may set out to construct a turn... for English [they] include sentential, clausal, phrasal, and lexical constructions" (p. 702). The first transition-relevance place for a turn is a likely location for turn-transfer, and if the current speaker has not pre-selected the next speaker (through eye-gaze, address term or other device), then other speakers may select themselves. When speakers self-select, it is predictable that the first to start will gain the floor, with other speakers dropping out; this rule is referred to as "first starter rights" (p. 704). There is also the possibility that the current speaker may self-select and continue talking after a possible completion point (if another does not self-select first).

The status of the first transition-relevance place, in combination with the first-starter rights to next turn, leads to the possibility of the turn-taking system exerting pressure on the size of turns. This pressure is characterized by Sacks *et al.* (1974) in the following way:

> ... the first-starter provision motivates any intending self-selector to start as early as possible at an earliest/next transition-relevance place; and a current speaker, oriented to that, will so construct a turn's talk as to allow its intact formation in the face of this pressure. Thus there is a pressure for turn-size minimization from both sides. (1974:719)[2]

Grammar can play a critical role in relation to the turn-taking system.[3] The size of the first turn-constructional unit can be increased through "internally generated expansions... BEFORE first possible completion places" (p. 709). In the following example, from my data, we can see the role of internal expansion in projecting a turn's completion beyond the limits of a single clause:

(2)
    V: An' also one more thing Mother wanted to know
→   whethe::r if we're going to the desert on

            the weekend, whether wu- we wanted to go to a (.)
            Halloween party they were gonna have.   (V 76)⁴

The conditional clause that is inserted after *whether* projects completion beyond itself (note that the completion of the embedded question is marked by the repetition of *whether* after the inserted *if*-clause). If the conditional clause were placed after its associated main clause, a transition relevance place would be reached before the condition was stated.

1.1.2 *Participants as sources for interpretations*

As mentioned above, an important principle governing the CA approach to conversation is the reliance on context and participant talk as sources for interpreting meaning. Levinson (1983) observes that:

> Conversation, as opposed to monologue, offers the analyst an invaluable analytical resource: as each turn is responded to by a second, we find displayed in that second an *analysis* of the first by its recipient. (321)

A simple example of using participants' talk as evidence for the meanings of utterances can be found in example 3. The context is an argument between a mother trying to get her son to go to bed, and the son wanting to convince his mother to let him stay up:

(3)
    M: I'm your mother.
    S: But it's Fri:day.

   A thorough CA account for this sequence would involve a turn-by-turn analysis of the interaction that led up to this particular exchange, but for the moment I want to concentrate merely on how these two turns suggest interpretations of previous talk. In the context of an argument, the mother's self-identification is a reminder of her special status as an authority figure, and it is also an indication that what has come before in the interaction has been behavior on the part of the son that did not fully acknowledge the mother's natural authority. Based on just this much analysis, we could look at the talk that preceded these two turns to see how the son's talk may have led to the interpretation of insubordination that we see his interlocutor providing.

The son's utterance, in the sequential slot after his mother's turn, is taken to be a response to her turn. His response is a further enactment of the argument sequence underway, the *but* reenforcing that the son's turn is to be taken as counter to what his mother has just said. We know, then, that the son's claim that the day is Friday is in some way a response to his mother's identification of herself as *mother*, and to her invocation of her authority. Adding to this a little knowledge of the cultural context, we can arrive at an interpretation of his utterance. Friday is an exceptional day with respect to sleep time since there is no school on Saturday.[5]

Thus, with the help of context: participants, talk and culture (which is what we all have access to as native-speaking interactants), we see how a simple act of identification (*I'm your mother*) can be treated as an invocation of authority, and how a simple identification of the day of the week (*But it's Friday*) can be taken as a questioning of the wisdom of that authority. We also see the way that the participants themselves can provide sources for the interpretation of their talk.

1.1.3 Sequential context

Conversations are structured sequences of turns. The smallest and most basic sequence is an *adjacency pair* (Schegloff and Sacks 1973). An adjacency pair consists of two turns, one party supplying the first pair part, and the other party responding with a second pair part. More precisely, a first pair part makes a second pair part "relevant," meaning that if, as is often the case, a question is not followed by a clear answer, whatever does follow will deal with the relevance of an answer. Some possibilities offered by Levinson (1983) are "partial answers, rejections of the presuppositions of questions," and "statements of ignorance" (293). Typical adjacency pairs are question–answer, greeting–greeting, and offer–acceptance/refusal (Schegloff and Sacks 1973:296).

The production of the first pair part of any adjacency pair type limits the options for what will follow it, and how what follows will be interpreted. Furthermore, among the types of utterances that one may produce after a particular first pair part, there is generally a preferred response. The designation "preferred" is not intended to entail an analysis of the psychological preferences of interactants. What CA scholars are predicting, through the claim that a preference structure is operating, is that a particular response will either be provided or be oriented to in some other manner. The behavior of participants displays an orientation to preference patterns. For example, many yes/no questions are built with a preference for an agreeing response. If such an answer is not forthcoming, there is regularly some hesitation or some other pre-indication that a "dispreferred" response is underway. Thus, the party delivering a second pair part, even when s/he is not supplying the preferred response, is oriented toward the existence of a preference. The speaker of a second pair part may "shape" her/his answer in orientation to the preferred agreeing response. This is done through initial or partial agreement, as well as through the softening of the disagreeing portion of the utterance (Sacks 1987).

In the following example, C, at 38, is checking her understanding of V's prior question. C produces the first pair part of a question–answer adjacency pair. V is not able to completely agree with C's proposed understanding. However, after what in this context serves as a marker of possible disagreement (*Well*), V shapes her response to be a modification of C's understanding rather than a bare disagreement.

(4)
```
35   V:   Okay this is what th-the problem is, my dad's
36        knee- leg is very bow-legged. It was like
37        thirt ⌈een degrees
38   C:         ⌊All his life. Right?
39   V:   Well:, more in old age(h).                    (K 35)
```

Here are two more examples offered by Levinson (1983) to illustrate the difference between preferred and dispreferred responses. Example 5 is characteristic of preferred responses in that the preferred agreeing response is given immediately without hesitation or delay.

(5)
```
Child:   Could you .hh could you put the light on for my
         room
Father:  Yep            (1983:307, attributed to Wootton, in press)
```

In contrast, example 6, involving a dispreferred response, exhibits delay (the pause after the first pair part), hesitation (*Ah um*), and finally the dispreferred content, *I doubt it*. Note that the dispreferred response is treated by its speaker as making an explanation relevant; R produces an account for why he is unable to agree to C's request.

(6)
> C: Um I wondered if there's any chance of seeing you tomorrow sometime (0.5) morning or before the seminar
>   (1.0)
> R: Ah um (.) I doubt it
> C: Uhm huh
> R: The reason is I'm seeing Elizabeth   (1983:308)

Through a variety of types of expansions, adjacency pairs are built into the larger sequences of turns in conversations. For example, C's question at line 38 in example (4) initiates an adjacency pair which becomes an insertion in the middle of the sequence already in progress. The sequence already in progress involves a question by C and a lengthy answer by V. V's turn at the beginning of this excerpt (line 35) is part of her response to the prior question by C. Similarly, in example (6), R's account of his reason for not agreeing with C's request is given in a post-expansion of the original adjacency pair. In this last example, a non-compliant response to a request has made relevant an account for the non-compliant or disagreeing response.

Other recurrent structures found in conversation, which are more complex than the basic adjacency pair, are openings and closings (Schegloff 1968, Schegloff and Sacks 1973), stories (Sacks 1972, Jefferson 1978), repair and correction sequences (Jefferson 1974, Schegloff, Jefferson, and Sacks 1977, Schegloff 1979), and topic introduction and change (Button and Casey 1984, Jefferson 1981), to name just a few well-examined patterns.

In all interpretation, the conversation analyst focuses on the placement of an utterance in a sequential slot. The principle of interpretation at work in all conversation analysis involves the notion of *conditional relevance*. Levinson (1983) explains that notion in the following way:

> [Conditional relevance is] the criterion for adjacency pairs that, given a first part of a pair, a second part is immediately relevant and expectable (Schegloff, 1972:363ff). If such a second fails to occur, it is noticeably absent; and if some other first part occurs in its place then that will be heard where possible as some preliminary to the doing of the second part... What the notion of conditional relevance makes clear is that what binds the parts of adjacency pairs together is not a formation rule of the sort that would specify that a question must receive an answer if it is to count as a well-formed discourse, but the setting up of specific expectations which have to be attended to. (1983:306)

Levinson's remarks with reference to adjacency pairs also hold with more complex interactional structures: certain utterance types are "relevant or expectable" in certain sequential environments.

The point which I would like to emphasize, then, in relating the sequential organization of conversation to the work at hand on adverbial clause usage, is that the occurrence of any utterance in conversation can be related to its prior context in terms of how it fills its sequential slot. CA provides an analytical tool for examining the sequential organization of any span of conversation. It also provides an independent body of findings on general tendencies and common interpretations of recurrent features of conversations (such as pauses, overlaps, questions followed by questions, stories, alignment and non-alignment of participants, etc.). Based on this approach, and the associated collection of prior findings, one can make claims about the way in which any particular turn addresses the relevant category of utterance or utterance types that might be expected at a given point in an unfolding sequence. Thus, any case of adverbial clause usage in my conversational corpus will be amenable to at least one reliable analysis, arrived at through CA methods. Instances of adverbial clause usage will be embedded in characterizable sequential contexts which will, to varying degrees, affect the interpretation of the interactional work performed by the clause.

1.1.4 *Summary of conversation analysis*

In this section, I have reviewed CA methodology and outlined some of the fundamental principles that have been found to operate in ordinary conversational interaction. The conversational turn-taking system is a model proposed to account for the occurrence of smooth and regular speaker change. It is crucial to the turn-taking system that interactants share an understanding of the grammatical and intonational resources of their language. In a CA approach, the conversational participants are seen as special resources for the interpretation of talk, and the sequential context of an utterance is vital to the determination of its meaning, the work that it is doing in the interaction. When gaps or troubles occur in interaction, the problems can be interpreted with reference to the operation of the turn-taking system, the talk of the participants themselves, and the characterizable sequential organization operating at the particular point in the conversation.

The principles outlined in this section will be relevant throughout the detailed discussion of occurrences of adverbial clauses in chapters 3 through 6.

1.2 Adverbial clauses in English discourse

In conversation, adverbial clause subordination is most commonly achieved through conditional, causal, and temporal conjunctions: *if, because, when, whenever, before, after, as,* etc. A number of studies, treating adverbial clauses as a group (Chafe 1984) or examining specific clause types (Linde 1976, Silva 1981, Thompson 1985b, Ford and Thompson 1986, Ramsay 1987, Schiffrin 1985, 1987), have focused on the discourse options associated with the property of "bidirectionality," i.e., the ability of clauses introduced by adverbial conjunctions to modify preceding material or material yet to come (Chafe 1988). These studies argue for a functional dichotomy between adverbial clauses which appear after the modified material and those which appear as a form of introduction to the material to be modified. These two positions are distinct in their roles in managing both the linear flow of information in a text and the attention of the listener (or, in writing, the reader) as it is guided through the text.

While none of the adverbial clause studies I review below, with the exception of the Schiffrin study (1985), treats, in any depth, the use of adverbial clauses in interaction, the findings are nonetheless relevant as they constitute the body of claims that exists to date on the discourse role of adverbial clauses in English. In the present study, I adapt these claims to conversational data, while at the same time placing a central focus on the interactional work that is accomplished through adverbial clause usage.

1.2.1 The functions of different adverbial clause types

Elaborating on the rather elusive notion of sentential "theme" in written English, Fries (1983) describes how the initial elements of sentences in written English can be understood as providing clues for the reader as to the method of development being used by the writer. One good example of the guiding function of non-subject sentence-initial elements is found in the spoken description of an apartment, taken from Linde and Labov (1975):

(7)
<u>As you open the door</u>, you are in a small five-by-five room which is a small closet.

<u>When you get past there</u>, you're in what we call the foyer which is about a twelve-by-twelve room which has a telephone and a desk.

<u>If you keep walking in that same direction</u>, you're confronted by two rooms in front of you... large living room which is about twelve-by-twelve on the left side.

<u>And on the right side</u>, straight ahead of you again, is a dining room which is not too big.

<u>And even further ahead of the dining room</u> is a kitchen which has a window in it. (1975:929–930)

Here we find some of the sentence-initial elements in the description of an apartment layout literally guiding the listener, spatially, through the apartment. By beginning each sentence with an element of spatial direction or movement, the speaker identifies each sentence as one in a series of sentences in a text which uses spatial orientation as its method of development. Similar orienting or guiding functions can be found in texts with other methods of development, such as procedural texts or essays of comparison and contrast. Initially placed adverbial clauses are prime examples of sentence-initial elements that do guiding and shifting work in the development of discourse.

Using Fries' insights on the discourse-orientational functions of initial elements in sentences as one point of departure, Thompson

(1985b), looking at written English discourse, questions the assumption that in actual use there is a discourse functional domain shared by initial and final adverbial clauses. Describing the use of purpose clauses, Thompson convincingly supports the claim that initial and final purpose clauses, "which share the same morphology, [...] behave in radically different ways in the organization of the discourse" (1985b:55). Thompson finds that, when a text is describing a problem, the problem is often encapsulated in the form of a purpose clause which, in its statement, sets up the expectation that a solution will follow. When a problem is encapsulated in a purpose clause, that clause appears before the clause or clauses that present the solution. An initial purpose clause may serve to introduce a solution that spans several clauses. Here is an example from Thompson's article of an initial purpose clause which encapsulates a problem and scopes over a number of clauses of solution. The passage is from *The Joy of Cooking*:

(8)
> (Section on "Carving Meat")... Keeping the knife blade sharp and under easy control is important. But of equal importance to the successful carver is keeping the V-edge true by the use of a steel. And the following procedure should precede the use of the knife before each carving period. The steel, which should be magnetized, realigns the molecular structure of the blade. *To true a blade*, hold the steel firmly in the left hand, thumb on top of handle. Hold the hand slightly away from the body. Hold the knife in right hand, with the point upward. Place the heel of the blade against the far side of the tip of the steel, as illustrated. The steel blade should meet at about a 15' to 25' angle. Draw the blade across the steel. Bring the blade down across the steel, toward the left hand, with a quick swinging motion of the right wrist. The entire blade should pass lightly over the steel... (1985b:64)

I quote some of Thompson's explication of this example:

> The text preceding the italicized purpose clause in this example is about sharpening a knife blade; the expectations which it raises, then, have to do with how to get the blade sharp, particularly with how to maintain equal angles on both sides of the "V" formed by the edge of the blade ("keeping the V-edge true"). Within that set of expectations, the purpose clause *To true a blade* names the obvious problem; the material following it provides the solution.
> (1985b:65)

In contrast to the function of initial purpose clauses, final purpose clauses serve to delimit the interpretation of only the immediate main clauses to which they are joined, and they do not respond to any expectation that a problem exists. They simply state the purpose or goal of some action in the main clause. Thompson illustrates this with an example from the description of an ocean voyage:

(9)
>George had always been my first choice for crew. Twenty-six years old, he had served in the army and later gone to the Middle East *to train soldiers for an oil rich sheik*. With the money saved from this venture, he had decided to take a couple of years looking around the world and pleasing himself. (1985b:68)

Thompson's explication of this example emphasizes the contrast with initial purpose clauses:

>Here there is nothing either in the text or derivable from it which creates any expectations within which training soldiers for an oil-rich sheik is a problem ... nor is any solution ever presented. This final purpose clause serves simply to state what George's purpose was for going to the Middle East. (1985b:68)

Although Thompson's study concentrates on written monologue, and the use of pre-posed purpose clauses is rare in conversation, her description of the use of such clauses in the organization of written discourse is relevant to the concerns of the present study. The discourse organizing function of initially placed adverbial clauses provides a point of reference and comparison for my study.

Unlike purpose clauses, conditional clauses are commonly found in initial position in conversational, as well as monologue, data. Looking at conditionals in English discourse, Ford and Thompson (1986) use written, as well as spoken, data to support the claim that the function of initially placed *if*-clauses in English is related to discourse properties associated with the notion of topic. This relationship was originally suggested by Haiman (1978) in a cross-linguistic, sentence-level study of the marking and function of conditional clauses. Ford and Thompson report that initial conditional clauses serve a general framework- or background-creating function for the discourse that follows them.

Introduction 15

If-clauses can be tied to the preceding discourse as highlighting some assumption, contrasting with an assumption, introducing an example, or exploring options. Ford and Thompson argue that an initial conditional clause

> brings a complex referent – explicit background information expressed in a clause – into the discourse. Whether an *if*-clause reiterates an assumption, makes a contrast, introduces a particular case or explores an option, it represents a limitation of focus and provides an explicit background for utterances which follow.
> (1986:370)

The semantics of hypotheticality make conditional clauses particularly useful for presenting a piece of information as at least temporarily "given," meaning that it is to be treated as shared background for the discourse that follows. Encoding information in a conditional clause creates a hedge, allowing for an alternative while assuming the temporary possibility of a situation for the span of talk that follows (see Brown and Levinson 1987:144 and Sweetser 1990:118–121).

A difference in the distribution of conditional as compared with purpose clauses, as mentioned above, is that, while purpose clauses are more likely to appear finally, *if*-clauses appear most commonly in initial position. This may be related to the fact that an *if*-clause can, speaking very broadly, present background for another clause or series of clauses. A purpose clause, on the other hand, has a more specific interpretation. Thus, the prevalence of initially placed *if*-clauses may reflect their general tendency to signal that some other clause is yet to come, and that the interpretation of the coming clause will be, in some general way, limited by the contents of the *if*-clause. As with purpose clauses, conditional clauses, when they appear sentence-finally, tend to have a much more limited scope, often modifying only some phrase or nominalization in the main clause.

Although the data for the Ford and Thompson (1986) study includes talk produced in interaction, there is little attempt to do any rigorous analysis of the interactional work that may characterize use of the structure.

The pattern of predominantly initial placement of *if*-clauses has been found in other discourse-based studies (Linde 1976, Ramsay

1987). Ramsay's findings, based on data from a novel, support the notion that initial *if*-clauses have a discourse organizational function. Ramsay uses quantification to support her claims, looking at, among other measures, the reference of subject NPs in conditional clauses relative to the preceding discourse. She finds that the subjects of initial *if*-clauses are referentially tied to a larger span of preceding text than are final *if*-clauses.

Ramsay (1987) also measures the continuity of subject NP reference as well as verb aspect patterns in initial versus final *when*-clauses in an English novel. Again, her counts indicate that initial *when*-clauses are tied to a larger span of the preceding text than are final *when*-clauses. Based on findings involving verb aspect variation, Ramsay suggests that "the information conveyed by . . . final *when*-clause[s] does not advance the main line of the narrative . . . it only completes the information given in the main clause" (1987:404). The participation of initial *when*-clauses in the presentation of main events in a narrative is seen as a part of the discourse organizational function of such clauses as opposed to final clauses.

Silva (1981) examines the occurrence of temporal connectives in a collection of controlled oral narratives, all based on responses to a set of pictures depicting ordered events. Silva reports that her respondents "tend to use preposed *when*-clauses to introduce a new frame." Initial *when*-clauses set the background for main events that are depicted in her picture story frames.

A study by Schiffrin (1985) describes aspects of the use of *because* in spoken English. Using a quantitative methodology, Schiffrin looks at "causal sequences." She operationalizes the notions of temporal sequencing and topic continuity in order to explain the choice between *so* and *because* as causal connectors.

While Schiffrin does not deal with the discourse organizational functions of adverbial clauses *per se*, she does note that the option of initial placement for *because*-clauses is essentially never taken in her corpus. She gives the following as the only pattern in which *because*-clauses appear before main clauses:

(10)
    I says, "You're a bum."
    Cause Bubby and Zede was here,
    I says, "You're no good."   (Schiffrin 1985:283)

Thus, cases of *because + consequence* are in fact *consequence + because + consequence* sequences, where the meaning of the consequent clauses is the same. It is never the case that a *because*-clause precedes the consequent clause without the same consequence having been stated previous to the causal clause. In my conversational corpus, *because*-clauses are never placed before the material they modify.

1.2.2 Adverbial clauses and intonation

While the studies reviewed above look at specific adverbial clause types in English, a study by Chafe (1984) examines English adverbial clauses as a group. Chafe finds that very few adverbial clauses appear initially under the same contour as their main clauses. He suggests that this pattern is compatible with the new information status of adverbial clauses. New information should appear either under its own contour or under the same contour as the main clause in the new information position, that is, after the main clause.

In a finding related to the possible interactional emergence of post-posed adverbial clauses, Chafe reports that, in his spoken data, such clauses often "occur as intonationally separate afterthoughts" (1984:448). I will suggest that naming the phenomenon of intonationally separate, post-posed adverbials "afterthoughts" focuses on the internal process of thinking of something additional to say, whereas the process may, in fact, either involve an internal evaluation of the interactional interpretability of prior talk, or be the result of some response or lack thereof on the part of a recipient; both cognitive and interactional motivations must be considered.

1.2.3 Summary: adverbial clauses in English discourse

The claims I have reviewed regarding the use of adverbial clauses in English discourse can be summarized as follows:

1. An initial adverbial clause does text-organizing work along with whatever semantic limitation, qualification or grounding it provides.

2. A final adverbial clause, especially when included under the same intonation contour as its main clause, is not involved in discourse-organizing work but is, instead, local in scope, merely providing semantic limitation, qualification or grounding for the one main clause to which it is related.
3. A final adverbial clause, when it follows the intonationally signaled closing off of the prior utterance (falling intonation plus pause), represents an "afterthought," something added to the prior utterance after its initial planning and production.
4. An initial adverbial clause, because of its text-organizing function, may have more than one of the subsequent clauses within its scope of limitation, qualification or grounding.

It is important to note again that none of the evidence for these claims, except for Schiffrin (1985), originates from a close look at the use of such adverbial clauses in contexts where, in addition to considerations of discourse organization, interactional functions are considered. As a means of addressing the evident gap in our knowledge, in the present study I have looked exclusively at conversational data with special attention to the interactional work that is done through the use of adverbial clauses.

1.2.4 Quantitative studies comparing speech and writing

Three additional studies that contain findings on the use of adverbial clauses require brief mention, as they provide further motivation for the current research. These studies call attention to the relative frequency of adverbial clauses in spoken English, and, at the same time, they point to our lack of understanding of what such clauses are doing in spoken data. In a study of "'Subordination' in formal and informal discourse," Thompson (1985a) counts several different kinds of grammatical dependencies, comparing their occurrence in samples of formal written, informal written, and informal spoken English. In the last category she specifically limits herself to monologues. Looking at the first 300 clauses in each corpus, she finds the following:

> 82% of the dependent clauses which appear in the Spoken Informal discourse data . . . are of the adverbial clause type. . . . Extrapolation from these figures suggests that almost all of the dependencies in

> Spoken discourse occur in the adverbial clauses, with people giving causal, conditional, and temporal comments on the events they are discussing. (1985a:91–92)

Thompson's paper is aimed at providing a more precise description of "subordination," a notion that has covered a composite of features which may be best looked at separately. She suggests that we must "try to determine what each of them [the component parts] is doing in different types of discourse" (1985a:93). We do not know what the component part of subordination most commonly used in spoken English (i.e., the adverbial clause) is actually doing there, especially spoken English in conversation.

Two other researchers, Beaman (1984) and Biber (1986), have done quantified comparisons of the use of different grammatical devices in various genres of English discourse. Both find more conditional adverbials and reason (causal) adverbials in speech than in writing (Biber 1986:409). In order to make inferences about the type of work being done by such structures, Biber depends on isolating the "function most commonly associated with each feature" (1986:388). However, while Biber includes conversational data in his corpus, his associations of forms with functions are taken from available research, and do not include qualitative studies of conversational data. Since he admits that his findings depend on an assumption that "there are relatively few underlying communicative functions in English discourse" (1986: 391–392), there is almost nothing we can extrapolate from his findings with regard to the work of adverbial clauses in conversation apart from their frequency. In reporting their findings, both Beaman and Biber point to the need for more qualitative analyses of the functioning of different linguistic features in different text types. Biber calls for "more detailed study" (1986:409), and Beaman points to the need for "in-depth analysis, both formal and functional" (1984:46). At a time when quantitative linguistic studies are flourishing, it seems crucial that such studies be supported by sound qualitative work.

In the findings from discourse-oriented studies of adverbial clauses in English, there is a good deal of evidence for the discourse organizational work of initial placement. However, no one has seriously looked at the work of adverbial clauses in conversation. In fact, quantitative studies looking at adverbial clauses across genres are notably uninformed with regard to the particular functions of adverbial clauses in interactional language use.

1.3 Chapter summary and overview of the book

In this chapter, I have offered an outline of the fundamental principles of conversation analysis, the approach that I use to arrive at interpretations of the interactional functions of adverbial clauses in my corpus. I have also reviewed linguistic research pointing to the discourse organizational functions of initially placed adverbial clauses, and studies observing the frequency with which adverbial clauses are used in spoken English. In the remainder of the book I will be concerned with how participants in interaction use adverbial clauses to manage information, and to manage their roles and the presentation of their social selves in conversation.

In chapter 2 I introduce my data and present a general overview of the distribution of adverbial clauses in the conversational corpus. In the next three chapters I present a detailed examination of the work that adverbial clauses do in these conversations. Chapter 3 covers the uses of adverbial clauses placed before their main clauses. Chapter 4 compares initial and final adverbial clauses, focusing on the use of final placement where the preceding clause ends in continuing intonation. And chapter 5 covers adverbial clauses that follow talk that has been both grammatically and intonationally signaled as complete.

In chapter 6 I make explicit comparisons with respect to the distribution and functions of different clause types; in addition I report on some findings related to variation in the usage of different clause types. In the final chapter I summarize my findings and discuss the implications of this type of work for both applied and general linguistics.

2

Overview of the conversational corpus

This chapter presents a brief overview of the database and the distribution of adverbial clauses within it.

2.1 The data

The database includes thirteen naturally occurring telephone, face-to-face, two party, and multi-party conversations. None of the interaction originates from interview or data-elicitation formats. In this way, special turn-taking formats were avoided. Twelve of the conversations are audio taped, and one particularly long span of talk comes from a video taped multi-party conversation. All the data used for this study are transcribed according to the conventions of conversation analysis (CA).[1] In each instance of an adverbial clause, I have done a careful analysis of intonation. In some cases, this has resulted in the addition of commas (level rising, incomplete intonation) or periods (final falling intonation) to the original transcriptions.

All the conversations are between adults, and all are in relatively casual situations: chatting on the phone, drinking beer on a picnic, visiting over crackers and cheese after a movie, or eating dinner. Eight of the recordings are of two-party telephone conversations, eliminating the question of non-verbal signaling for at least a portion of the data. Five of the conversations are face-to-face, multi-party interactions, in which the contribution of non-verbal cues will not be addressed in this study. There are a total of 33 different speakers in the conversations, 20 women and 13 men. The level of education of the participants has not been controlled for, although there is a preponderance of college-aged young people, as many of the recordings were originally collected for class assignments in CA courses. As this study is concentrating on the establishment of some basic findings on the use of adverbial clauses in conversation, no theoretical claims are made about the influence of level of education, gender, or relationships between participants. This is not to say that such factors do not influence adverbial clause use, as they obviously may, but rather that a concentrated investigation of such factors is beyond the scope of the present research.

The following is a list of the transcripts used in the study with a short description of the interactants:

1. *TG*. A telephone conversation between two girls in their early 20s. Audio. 16:15 minutes.
2. *SN-4*. A face-to-face, multi-party conversation primarily between three young women and one young man (with a short appearance of another young woman). The participants live in a college housing complex. Audio. 12:00 minutes.
3. *HG*. A telephone conversation between two young women. Audio. 19:30 minutes.
4. *AM*. A face-to-face, multi-party conversation between two married couples and another woman friend. The participants are all in their early 30s and are college educated or in graduate school. Audio. 6:15 minutes.
5. *V*. A telephone conversation between a brother and a sister, both in their 30s. Audio. 3:20 minutes.
6. *HD*. A face-to-face, multi-party conversation over dinner. Participants include two teenage girls and their mothers. Audio. 6:30 minutes.
7. *K*. A face-to-face, multi-party conversation between two women in their early 30s, very good friends, and one man in his mid-20s. Audio. 7:45 minutes.
8. *TS*. A very brief telephone conversation between acquaintances, a man and a woman who had arranged to share a ride to Syracuse. Audio. 2 minutes.
9. *AR*. A telephone conversation between two friends, a man and a woman around 30 years old. Audio. 6:20 minutes.
10. *YG*. A telephone conversation between two men around 30 years old. Audio. 5:20 minutes.

11. *JP*. A telephone conversation between two men in their 20s. Audio. 5:30 minutes.
12. *DBB*. A telephone conversation between two college students, a man and a woman. 5:30 minutes.
13. *AD*. A face-to-face, multi-party, outdoor conversation involving three couples. Most of the transcript is of a portion of the conversation in which the three men are the main participants. Video. 19:30 minutes.

The database is a sample of adult speakers of standard American English, and generalizations from the data are limited by this fact. There is, however, an advantage to using this type of data for my purposes. CA findings to date are largely based on conversations in English, and, as CA provides the primary analytical framework for my study, the database is clearly appropriate.

2.2 Types of adverbial clauses represented in the data

There were three requirements for a grammatical unit to be counted as an adverbial clause: (1) the grammatical unit had to have a subject and verb, (2) it had to be introduced by an adverbial conjunction, and (3) it could not be functioning as a subject or object of the main clause verb.

There were a total of 194 adverbial clauses in the corpus. Of these, all but three were either temporal (*before, after, since, when, while, whenever, every time*), conditional (*if*), or causal (*because, 'cause,* and *since*). The three exceptions were concessives (*although, even though*). There were 63 temporal clauses, 52 conditional clauses, and 76 causal clauses.

In principle, one can expect considerable semantic overlap to be found in the interpretation of these different clause types. Thus, conditionals may involve semantic connections that are also interpretable as causal, as in "If you heat water, it boils" (fabricated example). And the temporal conjunctions *when* and *whenever* have conditional uses, as in "When the sun is out, photosynthesis takes place" (fabricated example). However, such rather scientific uses of both clause types were not common in these conversations. As will be seen in the following chapters, differences in surface conjunctions correlate with different functions and contexts of use.

Table 1. *Distribution of adverbial clauses by position and type*

	Temporal	Conditional	Causal	Concessive	Total
Initial	21	26	—	1	48 (25%)
Final	40	18	75	2	135 (69%)
No main clause	2	8	1	—	11 (6%)
Totals	63	52	76	3	194 (100%)

Of the 194 adverbial clauses in the corpus, 48 or 25% were initial, 135 or 69% were final, and 11 or 6% were presented with no main clause. Of the initial adverbial clauses, 21 were temporal, 26 were conditional, and 1 was concessive. Of the final adverbial clauses, 40 were temporal, 18 were conditional, 75 were causal, and 2 were concessive. Adverbial clauses without main clauses were primarily conditionals.

Table 1 displays the frequencies of the different clause types in each pattern of occurrence: initial, final or without a main clause. Initial causals were notably absent in the corpus, a phenomenon that will be dealt with in chapter 4.

All of the initial adverbial clauses ended in continuing intonation contours. These cases, then, involved intonational, as well as grammatical, signals of more-to-come. The 135 final adverbial clauses were divided into cases in which the connection to the previous clause was made after the previous clause had ended in continuing intonation, and cases in which the previous clause ended in final intonation (rising question intonation or final falling intonation). Table 2 displays this division. Thirty-three out of 40, or 82%, of the final temporals followed continuing intonation. Twelve out of 18, or 67%, of the final conditionals followed continuing intonation. But less than half of the causals, 35 out of 75, or 47%, followed continuing intonation.

The most striking pattern that emerges from this last grouping is that causal clauses appear as separate, intonationally disconnected units much more often than do temporals and conditionals. More will be said regarding patterns of intonation and placement in the chapters that follow.

Table 2. *Final adverbial clauses by intonation and type*

Intonation	Temporal	Conditional	Causal	Concessive	Total
Continuing	33 (82%)	12 (67%)	35 (47%)	—	80
Final	7 (18%)	6 (33%)	40 (53%)	2	55
Totals	40 (100%)	18 (100%)	75 (100%)	2	135

2.3 Summary

This chapter has given a general picture of the type of data used in the study: ordinary two- and multi-party conversations between adult native speakers of American English. An overview of the distribution of adverbial clauses in the data has also been provided. Three primary types of clauses were well-represented in the corpus: temporal, conditional, and causal. In the next three chapters, I present analyses of the information management and social-interactional functions of adverbial clauses in the three most frequent placement patterns: initial, final after continuing intonation, and final after ending intonation. The initial overview I have presented here should provide a point of reference the reader may return to while reading the more detailed discussions in chapters 3 through 6.

3

Initial adverbial clauses

In the present conversational corpus, initial adverbial clauses can be described in terms of the information patterns they form, and in terms of the interactional functions they serve. While the dichotomy between the information management or patterning and interactional functions of language is not a discrete one, there is value in approaching the description of adverbial clause usage with this division in mind. Because previous studies of adverbial clause usage have focused on monologue data, we know the kind of work such clauses do in less interactive discourse. That work has been described mainly in terms of information management. Prior studies have consistently pointed to a shift function for initial adverbial clauses. In monologue texts, such clauses set off prior discourse from discourse that follows. An initial adverbial clause uses information that has either appeared in some form in the previous discourse, or that follows sequentially from a point in the previous talk. Such information is either taken directly, negated or put in a contrasting form, or simply introduced as a possible option. The adverbial clause then constitutes explicit background for the following discourse.

With those findings as a source of comparison, we can look at the occurrence of adverbial clauses in conversation to see what such clauses do in encoding and organizing information and, additionally, in managing and maintaining interaction and the social roles of parties in conversations. It is assumed that information patterns, relations of these clauses to their textual environments, exist in conjunction with the interactional work that is being done at any point in a conversation. That is, the development of information patterns and the doing of interactional work are simultaneous processes. When I describe what I term the more interactional work of adverbial clauses, I refer to the work that such clauses do in addition to the message level information they convey or the information strategies they represent. In particular, when I speak of interactional work, I refer to the management of the direction of the conversation, the roles of the parties in the conversation, and the connection of talk across speakers rather than across utterances without reference to their speakers.

I emphasize again, as in chapter 1, that, in all discussions of the interactional work of adverbial clauses, special care is taken to use evidence from the surrounding conversational context and the interpretations of the participants themselves in order to arrive at interactional functions for the clauses in question. The interpretation of each adverbial clause is founded on, and supported by, a close reading of the interactional sequence in which it is used.[1]

3.1 Overview

All the initial adverbial clauses in the corpus are intonationally continuous with the material they modify, that is, none is separated from its modified material by final falling intonation. Intonationally, then, initial adverbial clauses are presented as incomplete in themselves, and as subparts of larger units – to be interpreted along with material yet to come.

Initial adverbial clauses make up 24% (48) of the total adverbial clauses in the data. Another 11 clauses that appear without main clauses are also included in the present discussion, as they share functional properties with initial adverbial clauses. Thus, this chapter addresses the discourse and interactional functions of 59 (28%) of the clauses in the data base.

Of the 48 initial adverbial clauses with main clauses, 21 are temporal clauses, clauses introduced by *when, whenever, every time, by the time, before, after,* etc., 26 are conditional clauses,

Table 3. *Initial adverbial clauses*

Temporal	Conditional	Concessive	Total
21	26	1	48

introduced by *if*, and there is one initial concessive clause, introduced by *rather than*. As noted in chapter 2, causal clauses do not appear before their main clauses; they will be covered in chapters 4 and 5.

3.2 The work of initial adverbial clauses

The remainder of this chapter is divided into sections according to the different discourse work that initial adverbial clauses do in the corpus. The presentation is organized around the following three categories of function: temporal shift, choice among options, and contrast. Each section describes the ways in which initial adverbial clauses pattern in terms of these information relations, each adverbial clause forming an explicit tie to previous discourse, and providing an explicit frame for the discourse that follows. Each section also describes the role of initial adverbial clauses in interaction, focusing on particular ways in which the information patterns are associated with strategies of interaction.

3.2.1 Introducing and shifting time frames: temporal clauses

It is usually possible to determine, at any given point in a conversation, what the time reference is. Just as pronoun reference must be introduced and shared by speakers, so time reference is a domain of talk that requires management and attention on the parts of conversational participants.[2] Time reference may be generic or specific. It may be shifted from generic to specific, from one specific time to another, from one generic time to another, or from specific to generic.

One common use of initial temporal clauses is for the presentation of time frames in reports of sequenced events. Initial temporal clauses establish temporal or situational frames for assertions that follow. They are commonly used to create shifts in time, from a time frame already operating in the talk to the time frame introduced by the adverbial clause itself. In the telling of a story or the description of habitual sequenced activities, time frames are regularly established and changed through initial temporal clauses.

The following example involves an initial *when*-clause that sets

Initial adverbial clauses

up the situational frame for a description of the celebration of a Nepali's seventy-seventh birthday:

(1)
```
         W:   Well what made you the si:ckest.
              (1.0)
         C:   You could never ⎡identify it.
         D:                   ⎣Mm:
         H:   =You don't kno:w. Ye:ah
    →    D:   =No I know. I('d be) pretty sure it was when-
              (0.8)
    →    D:   I went to this thing,
              (1.0)
    →    D:   When a pe(r)- when a ol:d man reaches seventy
              seven, they have this big ceremony, (i wu)s
              like his rebir:th or, something. An' they do wha-
              they (.) carry him on his ba:ck, n' put him in a
              chariot, n' (.) carry him around all the (.)
              ki:ds drag him around through the village, an'
              stuff (they do all this) the(n'they have a) big
              fea:st, an' they drink, they have these bi:g (.)
              jars full of this (.) mm- (1.0) it's like
              fermenten:ted wi(n) or- fermented ri:ce. It's like
              (.) they (.) y'know rice-
         W:   Rice wine?                                    (AM 123)
```

In example 1, D cuts himself off (at the first arrow) and then continues (second arrow). It could be that at this point D has realized that the situation in which he got *the sickest* cannot be condensed into a short turn. The vagueness in the expression *thing* in the clause which follows the cut-off projects more elaboration. In fact, as will be seen in several other cases discussed below, *thing* can be seen as involved in a practice of speaking whereby a semantically broad form is used cataphorically to project an upcoming, more elaborate explication. Just following the clause *I went to this thing*, there is a one second pause. This comes at a point of possible completion, i.e., another speaker could talk here. The fact that no one else comes in shows that D has succeeded in projecting an extended turn.[3] The initial *when*-clause at the third arrow marks the beginning of a reported sequence of events, giving the time and situational frame in which the following event sequence takes place. The initial temporal clause comes, then, at a point in the talk when an explicit time frame has not been established; the *when*-clause creates a time frame and initiates the explication of the generic *thing* referred to earlier.

The information pattern here has clear interactional significance. The introduction of a semantically broad term projects explication, and the beginning of the explication is marked by a change from no time frame to a general time frame, introduced in the form of an initial *when*-clause. What is introduced and temporally framed by D's initial *when*-clause is his presentation of the generic event sequence in which he participated and which made him *the sickest*. The projection of an extended turn, in this case a story, has interactional consequences in terms of the type of work the recipients are expected to do to facilitate the telling. Recipients facilitate the extended turn by not treating grammatical completion as a signal of turn completion. They also take specific types of turns while the story is being told. They produce continuers, repair initiators, and provide help in word searches, as when W offers *Rice wine?* (last line of example 1).

In the next example, an initial temporal clause is again used to introduce an event in a time sequence not present in the prior talk. Here the shift is from one time to a new time, the new time topically, but not temporally, coherent with the first. The example comes from a discussion of problems with teenagers. N and B are mothers eating dinner with their teenage daughters, E and L. They have been talking about the problems of another family. At the first arrow, N brings up a time in her own life as an example. At the second arrow, N moves from a generalization to a specific event, introduced by an initial *when*-clause:

(2)
  (*It* refers to the problems with the family.)
  N: They couldn't (.) they couldn't have any kind of normal communication.
  B: Yeah you can't work it out, you can't negotiate,
       (1.0)
  N: It STA:RTed because Ann refused to accept the boyfriend.
  L: I can understand that,
→ N: Yeah. I can understand both sides, I've been both plac(h)es.
       (1.0)
→ N: I mean (.) when I really (.) didn't want Brian around,
       (1.0)
  N: It was hell here.=

```
E:  =Did Abbey leave?
L:  You didn't (feel) Abbey's ⎡side during the:n.
                              ⎣°No.
N:  I did fee- ah what I felt is I pushed Abbey to the wa:ll. So that
    she was always unhappy.                              (HD 161)
```

This piece of talk is similar to example 1 in that the initial temporal clause introduces the case that provides supportive details or an elaboration of the speaker's immediately prior assertion. In example 1, D asserts that he knows when he got the sickest, and his initial *when*-clause marks the beginning of the event that made him sick. In example 2, N asserts that she can understand both sides of the issue at hand, and her initial *when*-clause introduces the case that demonstrates her understanding. N's talk involves an initial *when*-clause that forms a shift from commentary and generalization originating from talk about a past time, to a specific past time that serves to introduce a more specified account in support of the previous generalization.

Note also that N's move to a specific example follows an interactionally significant one second pause. N's generalization is treated as warranting elaboration, and the other conversational participants allow N to go on to explicate it. This, then, is an interactionally negotiated turn extension, with the extension introduced by an initial adverbial clause.

Initial *when*-clauses are not only used to set up the initial time frames for event sequences or to move from one time frame to a wholly different one, they are also used *within* event sequences to create shifts in time and situation as part of the reporting of one continuous sequence. While example 2 displays a shift from a generalization to a specific time frame, in the next two examples we find cases of initial *when*-clauses expressing time frame shifts within reports of specific sequenced events.

In example 3, J is explaining to P why J's roommate is angry at J. The anger arose from the events of a prior evening when J helped create friction between his roommate and his roommate's potential girlfriend, who was a dinner guest. Here, J is reporting the problematic chain of events. He uses an initial *when*-clause to move from the time when his roommate was fixing dinner to the time when his roommate and guest were eating:

(3)
```
      J: He: was all excited, 'cause he's having this girl Do:nna, over
         for dinner.
      P: Mh hum.
      J: 'n he made dinner 'n all that, she showed up and she's a funny
         girl .hh (0.4) So I was talkin' to her, while he was making
→        dinner, an' then, (0.7) .hhh um (0.4) w-when they were eating,
         (0.4) she mentioned something, about his spaghetti, being stuck
         together, an' so we started picking on him and his food, .hhh
         (0.2) and went on from there, it just snowballed into Donna
         an' I just had the best time picking on him ah .hhh (0.2)
         having fun,                                          (PJ 4.15)
```

As in example 1, where the word *thing* served as a semantically broad term projecting elaboration, the initial *when*-clause in 3 comes as an explication of the temporal deictic *then*. This temporal deictic functions in a manner similar to *thing*, in that its reference is made explicit in what follows. J's initial *when*-clause elaborates on the reference of the prior *then*. The *then* marks a sequentially next time in the event chain, and the initial *when*-clause that follows specifically introduces the situational and temporal frame in which some of the more significant events took place, the actions that frustrated J's roommate. Note that the temporal framework introduced by the *when*-clause holds for several clauses that follow, that is, there is an extended scope for this initial adverbial clause. That initial adverbial clauses tend to have greater scope than final adverbial clauses has been observed in studies from written data as well (Thompson 1985b, Ramsay 1987).

In example 4, below, a similar pattern is evident. M is reporting the events that led to a big fight at the car races the night before this conversation. In the talk previous to this point, the main characters in the story have been introduced. De Wald is the antagonist, who seemingly without provocation goes after Keegan:

(4)
```
      M: De Wa::ld spun ou:t. 'n he waited. (0.5) Al come around 'n
         passed him, Al was leadin' the feature, (0.5) an' then the
→        second place guy, (0.8) an' then Keegan. An' boy when Keegan
         come around, he come right up into him, tried to put him into
         the wa:ll.
      C: Yeh?
```

Initial adverbial clauses

M: 'n he tried it about four different times, finally Keegan rapped him a good one in the a:ss, 'n then th- b- DeWald went o:ff.
(AD 10.12)

In this span of talk, M describes De Wald as waiting while the other competitors come around the track. Al comes around and is followed by the second-place driver, and *then Keegan*. Again a *then* marks a time which is immediately respecified in the initial *when*-clause, *when Keegan come around*. Keegan's arrival is a shift point leading to De Wald's aggression. This is highlighted by the *An' boy* exclamation that precedes the *when*-clause. The *when*-clause, then, gives the specific temporal and situational background for the next significant event in the story. This new time frame, beginning *when Keegan come around*, serves as the backdrop for several clauses to follow. Note that the arrival of Keegan, introduced by an initial *when*-clause, receives a recipient response: C's *yeh*. This is an interactionally important achievement, involving the explicit signaling of what the recipient should take as a special event. Thus, the initial *when*-clause both presents information and participates in the signaling of a high point in the story, a point which invites a recipient response.

In the next example, from the conversation about the auto races, G makes three shifts in time frame. The first is not achieved through an adverbial clause. The second and third, while both done through initial adverbial clauses, are used to perform different types of shifts and have different interactional implications.

The excerpt begins as G has been talking about a time in the past when he frequented the race track. M comments that that was long ago, and G confirms this. G then very explicitly moves to the present time, at the first arrow. He does this not through an adverbial clause, but by a more cumbersome method: the first part of his sentence closes the previous time, *I used to go over there the:n*, and the same sentence continues to introduce the new time, *n' no:w, Rich Hawkins from Bellview drives one*. Then, after a span of talk about Hawkins, who races at the present time, that line of talk reaches a lapse at the four-second pause (line 23). G then moves back to the past time. To mark the beginning of talk about past events, G uses an initial temporal clause (second arrow). Notice that this initial adverbial, as that in example 1 above, begins the telling of a sequence of events:

(5)
```
          2   G:   Sam's from Bellview. He had a Oh two. It was a,
          3        modified. Six cylinder::?
          4   M:   Oh yeah th⎡at's goin' way ba:ck.
          5   G:         ⎣(That's a lo:ng time ago).
          6   G:   That was a lo:ng time a⎡go.
          7   M:                          ⎣Yeah.
          8        (1.0)
  →       9   G:   I used to go over there the:⎡n 'n, no:w, Rich=
         10   M:                               ⎣((clears throat))
         11   G:   =Hawkins from Bellview drives one, for some guys
         12        from up't Bellview.
         13        (0.4)
         14   M:   Yah.
         15   G:   He's my:: little sister's brother'n law.
         16        (0.5)
         17   G:   He's a policeman in Bellview but he- (0.4) I guess
         18        he's, not afraid to drive a ca:r,
         19        (1.0)
         20   G:   I d'know what they have to dri:ve I haven't even
         21        been over to see (im⎡lately)
         22   M:                       ⎣It's a pretty good ca:r.
         23        (4.2)
  →      24   G:   Every time I went over there I froze m'nu:ts.
         25        (1.0)
         26   M:   .hh hh ⎡hh!
         27   G:          ⎣You always go over en ni- nice in the
         28        afternoon an' you go over there wi⎡th jus::]t=
         29   M:                                     ⎣Yeah.]
         30   G:   =shirtsleeves on or just a, short sleeve shirt'n
  →      31        'fore the night is over you're freezin' t'death.
         32        You're not allowed t'dri:nk,
         33   M:   Hawkins the one that hit Al last year over in
         34        Finley an',
         35        (1.0)
         36   M:   flipped him'n put Al in that bad accident.
         37   G:   Wzee
         38   C:   Oh really?
         39   M:   Yah.
         40        (2.0)
         41   C:   °Al's a pretty damn good driver. He's been around
         42        for a little while,
         43   M:   Yeah. Al? He's been around thirteen years.
                                                           (AD 18–19)
```

Whereas the temporal clause at the second arrow marks a shift to a new time frame entirely, the temporal clause at the third arrow marks a shift within a developing sequence of events. G's *every time* moves from a general present time frame to general past and introduces a story, a story about how cold it was at the track ("I froze my nuts."). His *'fore the night is over* moves the developing story to its completion, the point at which the "freezing" is reported.

These two clauses are similar in that they form shifts in the current, default time setting, specifying new temporal backgrounds for the talk that follows. However, there is more going on in this talk than just the changing of temporal settings. These two clauses participate in different ways in the interactional work in this stretch of talk. The temporal clause at 31 forms a shift in temporal setting within a longish turn, wherein the talk is controlled by one party. Taking 24–32 as a unit, 24 projects a particular kind of outcome for the story that follows: that you freeze when you go to the races in the town in question. Lines 27 through 30 describe what, given the projection of freezing weather, must be taken as the initial weather condition. At line 31, introduced by the initial temporal clause *'fore the night is over*, the expected outcome is delivered. Thus, this initial adverbial clause both introduces a time frame change within the presentation of sequenced events and, in terms of interaction, marks the conclusion of this story as projected at line 24.

In contrast to the adverbial clause at 31, which appears near the culmination of a long turn, the adverbial clause at 24 appears turn-initially, with the immediately prior talk coming from another party. Furthermore, the shift introduced by this clause is a shift in both time and topic. The talk from lines 9 to 22 involved the identification of Hawkins and the car he drives, while G's shift at 24 gives up Hawkins as a central character in his talk and moves to the broader theme of the race track, his access to knowledge of it, and his basically negative experience there.

Relevant to this more global shift is the interactional fact that G has just, rather unsuccessfully, tried to show his knowledge of the track by reference to drivers he knows or has known there. In line 2, G mentions another driver he knew and Mike responds by placing that driver *way back in time*, not of current importance or interest. G's subsequent introduction of Hawkins, a driver he knows now, is also poorly received. In fact, M provides only minimal recognition: the *Yah* at 14, and G's increments of identification at 15 and 17 get no verbal acknowledgement. Some of the alternative second pair parts that might follow reports such as G's (9–12) would be utterances displaying interest or more clear recognition. M's *Yah* may just be signaling that he has heard G's talk. It is not until G mentions the car that M explicitly displays clearly that he knows exactly to whom G is referring. M even jumps in with his evaluation of the car slightly before the projected end of G's turn (line 22). This jumping in can be interpreted as an emphasized display of recognition, as though to say that M knew all along who G was referring to (which, in fact, is true; see discussion below).[4]

Significantly, it is after M's evaluation of the car and the long pause that follows that recognition that G introduces his temporal and topical shift, a move in which G is responding to his problematic interactional circumstances. There are at least three aspects of M's responses to G's talk before line 23 that add up to a display of minimal interest. M does not specifically respond to the introduction of Hawkins into the conversation. His evaluation of the car is delivered in such a way as to say, "I already know who you're talking about." And he does not attempt to add anything to the conversation during the interactionally remarkable four-second pause which follows his evaluation of the car. These unencouraging responses to talk about Hawkins seem to indicate an "abandonable" topic. Matters of face are at issue, and G's conversational competence is in question.

G's shift at 24, then, addresses the interactional problem of a failing topic. It should be clear as he shifts away from the present setting to the past that he has abandoned the present discussion of Hawkins, a current driver, for a different, hopefully more fruitful, line of talk.

M's attitude toward Hawkins and M's lack of interest in Hawkins as a positive topic of talk become clearer in lines 33–43[5]. Also, in the talk that leads up to this sequence, Al, the driver who was badly injured by Hawkins the year before, has been mentioned as the winner of the previous night's race. G's lack of success in introducing Hawkins as a favorable subject of talk is certainly related to Mike's poor opinion of Hawkins.

The two initial temporal clauses in example 5, then, participate in distinct ways in their interactional context. The clause at line

Initial adverbial clauses

31, introducing a shift in time in sequenced events, marks the expected outcome of a story as projected at 24. The adverbial clause at line 24, while also analyzable as a shift in temporal frame, is doing a different kind of interactional work by moving the talk away from a failing topic.

Time frame shifts may also move from specific to more generic reference. In the next example, C has just informed E that he cannot make the drive they had planned together. Here, near the close of the short telephone conversation, E makes the suggestion that she and C can make plans for another time. The first *when*-clause E uses is a final one (line 22), and the time reference in that clause is somewhat ambiguous. It does not refer to any unique agreed upon time in the future, but it could be interpreted as containing an element of expectation that a specific time will occur. The second adverbial clause (line 24), this one initial and introduced by *whenever*, is less ambiguous. *Whenever* can only be interpreted as referring to a non-specific time. Here, then, the movement in time reference is from a time that is indeterminate between non-specific and specific reference to a time that is distinctly non-specific.

(6)
```
      5   C:   Yihknow I really don't have a place to sta:y.
      6   E:   .hh Oh:::::.hh
      7        (0.2)
      8   E:   .hhh So yih not gonna go up this weekend?
      9   ( ): (hhh)
     10   C:   Nu::h I don't think so.
     11   E:   How about the following weekend.
     12        (0.8)
     13   C:   .hh That's the vacation isn't it?
     14   E:   .hhhhhh Oh:. .hh ALright so:- no ha:ssle,
     15        (.)
     16   E:   s⌈o-
     17   C:    ⌊Ye:h,
     18   E:   Yih kno:w::
     19   ( ): .hhh
     20   E:   So we'll make it for another ti:me then.
     21        (0.5)
     22   E:   Yih know just let me know, when you're gonna go:.
     23   C:   .hh Sure .hh
→    24   E:   yihknow that- that's all, whenever you have
```

25   intentions of going, .hh let me know.
26   C: Ri:ght.   (TS 2:8–25)

The interactional work here is a toning down of the original suggestion. In a negotiation to reach a sense of agreement, E backs off from the potential specificity of her reference to future plans. As can be seen from E's turn at 11, she had some hope of rescheduling the trip for a specific other time. C, however, was not forthcoming in helping arrange an alternate plan; note the pauses at lines 12 and 15, where C could have helped facilitate other plans. When, at line 20, E moves away from mentioning specific times and simply says they can make it for *another* time, it is not clear how much she really expects another plan to ever materialize. After a pause in which C gives no response, E makes an indirect offer through a directive, softened with *just*. She asks C to let her know when he is going to make the trip. This is where she makes the ambiguous time reference mentioned above, *when you're gonna go*. After C gives a minimal response (line 23), E recasts and tones down her offer. This time she shifts to a clearly non-specific time reference; to do this she uses an initial temporal clause preceded by *that's all*, another signal that she is diminishing or toning down the offer/directive. Note also the contrastive stress on *whenever*, marking it as a revision of *when* in E's previous turn. This toned-down offer is the culmination of a progressive backing off that E achieves beginning at line 8, when E first displays her understanding that the originally planned trip is off.

E first offers specific alternative plans, then retreats to a vague and ambiguous plan for the future, and finally has to make the non-specific nature of the future plan doubly explicit through the initial adverbial clause at the arrow. In this context, then, an initial adverbial clause, which creates a shift in time reference, is used interactionally to tone down an offer and to make it clear to the offer recipient that no obligation is intended.

In example 7, a last example of a time frame shift, we again find an initial temporal clause working at the information level to move the discourse from a specific time to generic time. The time frame changes from a more or less designated real time to a general or habitual time, i.e., a non-specific time. This case is from a conversation between three friends. V has been reporting on her father's need for a knee operation. She is recounting a particular occasion when the doctor was informing the family about the operation:

(7)
```
137   V: ...he said we'll probably have to put an
138      artificial knee in in five yearss.
139          (0.2)
140   V: For my dad.
141   C: °Hmm=
142   V: Because his knee'ez is deteriorating an' weak.
143   C: An' especially after they did the surgery an' saw
144      what it looked like? or
145   V: N-n:⎡o: they can jus- the xray or whatever.
146   C:    ⎣There's just not enough (left),
147   V: ⎡They can just see.
148   C: ⎣(I mean) your mom's weird.
149   V: So then .hh I was the:re, I was there. I heard it,
150      doctor knew what he was talking about, made my dad
151      feel comfortable, said that he's- gonna have this
152      sa:me operation, when he's- in about (0.2) twenty
153      years, cause he had bad knees from football, n-in
154      high scho⎡ol.
155   C:        ⎣Mm
156   V: An' he's about thirty five an' r⎡eal-
157   C:                                 ⎣You mean when
158      you get bad knees, yer- a- legs start automatically
159      guh- or you have to get a- a new knee cap, there
159a     or somethin'.
160   V: Yeah, but he was gonna have this first.⎡just like
161      my dad                                 ⎣
162   C:                                        ⎣Really?
163   V: This thing.
164   C:     (0.2)
165   V: Wedge thing.
166          (0.3)
167   V: An' his specialty is artificial knees. .hh So I
168      was there-
169          (0.2)
170   V: Made sense, I was calm, felt confident in the
171      doctor, he's a professor at USC,
172   C: °Mm hm                               (K 137–170)
```

In asking her question at line 157, C moves the time frame from a specific occasion, which has been the time frame of V's talk, to generic time. C's initial *when*-clause incorporates information mentioned in the prior talk, i.e., the need for knee operations because of bad knees. The *when*-clause presents that information in a generic form, using the impersonal *you* and a verb expressing present habitual time.

This shift in time reference coincides with C's attempt to make an interactional shift. To understand the interactional significance of C's *when*-clause at 157, we must look at the larger context. It is important to know that V's talk was originally prompted several transcript pages earlier when her boyfriend K complained about V's response to her mother. K believes that V's mother is overly worried and that V is overreacting to her mother's anxiety. In that context, C (V's good friend) asks V what her own first-hand knowledge of the severity of the father's operation is, *Have you met his doctor?* Through this question, C gives V the opportunity to explain *her* experience of the situation. This is an interactionally safe move for C, caught as she is between her friend and her friend's boyfriend.

V's talk originates, then, in an implication by her boyfriend that V's mother was overreacting to the operation and that V was overreacting to her mother. In the more local context, V seems to be trying to establish that her mother does not, in fact, have a good basis for being so worried. But, having asked the question that prompted V's talk, C attempts to regain control of the direction of the talk.

As evidence for C's role in trying to move the talk out of V's extended explanation, let me draw attention to one of C's turns, prior to the *when*-clause in question. C's talk in this turn diverges from the direction V is taking in her extended turn. After what seem to be appropriate displays of understanding at lines 141, 143, and 146, C interjects a comment on V's mother, line 148. The comment that V's mother is *weird* is not directly relevant to V's talk at this point in the conversation. Instead, it harks back to the origin of V's extended turn, that is the question of whether her mother was overreacting to the operation. Thus, C's comment here can be seen as an attempt to curtail V's extended turn, and to mark the story as having made its point. While V is in the middle of explaining the details of her father's knee condition and the doctor's prognosis, C jumps to a premature assessment of V's mother. Instead of curtailing V's talk, however, C's comment, which is in overlap with V's, is not acknowledged by V. C's comment, thus, has no visible interactional consequence.

C has attempted, then, to move the talk out of the extended explanation sequence, and this is relevant to the interactional work done by the initial *when*-clause at line 157–158. In the context of the extended explanation and C's move to get out of that line of talk, the initial *when*-clause at line 157 can be seen as not only introducing a shift from specific to generic time, but also as serving an interactional function related to the assessment cited above: the time frame shift is another attempt to take the talk in another direction.

At line 157, C does an understanding check that at the information level forms a shift away from the time reference in V's talk. The understanding check and movement to generic time become a further vehicle for C's attempt to regain control of the talk and bring V's extended turn to a close. C's turn moves away from the immediate focus of V's talk, on the trustworthiness of the doctor, to the general implication with regard to knees. V, however, does not incorporate C's shift into her response. V acknowledges C's question, but then elaborates by referring again to the specific doctor and the specific past time of their conversation. *Yeah, but he was gonna have this first.* In not responding in generic time, V successfully maneuvers around C's attempt to control the talk. So unlike the case of C's earlier attempt to curtail the talk above, V *does* respond here to C's turn, but V still maintains the continuity of her extended turn, and C remains in an extended recipient role. We see, here, that initial temporal clauses can be used interactionally in attempts to curtail an extended turn and shift the general direction of the talk.

Let me summarize what I have presented here regarding the use of initial temporal clauses. We have seen that initial temporal clauses in conversation, as in monologue, operate to provide temporal background for accounts, to encode new time frames within accounts of ordered events, and to move from specific to generic time frames. In a practice that leads into time frame shifts, semantically broad terms such as *thing* or *then* may be followed by explications beginning with initial *when*-clauses. The use of such terms contributes to the projection of extended turns and a modification of speaker–recipient roles.

In addition to using initial temporal clauses to introduce extended turns, interactants in these conversations use such clauses to mark the outcome of a story, to move talk away from a failing topic, to tone down the specificity of an offer, and to disrupt another person's hold on the floor by introducing a time reference different from that in a coparticipant's extended turn.

3.2.2 Presenting options: conditional clauses

At certain points in the unfolding of information in talk, especially, though not exclusively, information that concerns events or actions that have not yet occurred, speakers present options: possible situations, with possible outcomes contingent on particular options being taken. In the present data, as in the written and spoken data analyzed by Ford and Thompson (1986), initial *if*-clauses are commonly used as a strategy for presenting options. The options usually follow logically from a point reached in the previous talk. And even when they seem unexpected as options, they are being treated as possibly true at that point in the talk.

Here is an example of the presentation of an option through an initial *if*-clause. J is reporting a past conversation in which an option is expressed through an initial *if*-clause (at the arrow):

```
(8)
       J: He made one big mistake though, he insulted her intelligence.
       P: .Hhh
       J: And she (goes) I can't believe you said that and
          ⌈so::
       P: ⌊Oooh (Whu'd he do,) Oh:, O:K: now, well then if he: if
          he put his own foot in his ⌈mouth,
       J:                            ⌊Oh Oh, he did=he said, she said
          something that was really simplistic. I forget what it was, .hhh
          He goes, Ooo::, you are so smart, what were you, a cheer-
          leader in highschool?
       P: ⌈.hhh Ooo:::
       J: ⌊.hhh an' she goes I can't believe you said that
       P: Oooh:⌈
       J:     ⌊and so I (sd) I can't believe he said that either..hh
```

Initial adverbial clauses

→   an', I said, well, I'm leaving now=If you wanna go home, Donna, I'll take you.
P: .hh Oh::⸢::
J: ⸤hahaha .hhh
J: So ⸢she::: haha .hh
P: ⸤JO::HN
J: She: picked ⸢you up her ahahaha
P: ⸤You are puttin' SALT in the wound.
J: .hhh She picked up her books, put away her stuff .hh an' started to walk out the door with me, but then she said, No, I'm only teasing and went back .hh Butuh, (0.2) yeah, from that point on he was REally upset. .hhh
P: John, I'd be pissed too.   (PJ 8.8)

In example 8, the information in J's talk arrives at a point at which an option is presented as available: because J is leaving, Donna can get a ride home with him. The option *If you wanna go home*, appears as an initial *if*-clause. This clause is related to the prior discourse in that it encodes a contingency or possibility that becomes available at the point reached in the prior discourse (in this case, the reported interaction).

The strategy of presenting an option through an initial *if*-clause has the interactional significance of displaying an interpretation of prior talk. The conditional, *If you wanna go home*, proposes an option that is not obviously predictable from the context. By suggesting that the guest might want to leave, J is displaying an interpretation of his roommate's actions: that they were so damaging that the guest would want to leave. While the option of the guest leaving is meant to be an outrageous suggestion, the initial *if*-clause is in the familiar format of an option tied to previous talk. It is used to provide an extreme interpretation of the prior events. The joke comes in because the option is being treated as somehow normally arising, when in fact the suggestion is unexpected. That the option is really meant to be humorous is attested by the fact that the guest plays along with the joke by picking up her books, but later says she was only teasing.

In the next example, again involving an option, V and B, sister and brother, are making plans for B's visit. B will be arriving at V's apartment later that evening. He will be stopping at a friend's house on the way:

(9)
```
      B: So:, I'll-I'll probably leave there, at the latest ten, so I'll
         probably be there, at the latest ten- so I'll probably, be there
         at your place, at the latest midnight.
      V: Yea:h.
         (0.2)
  →   V: Shyoo! .hhh Okay, well if I go to bed, I'monna leave the door
         open.
      B: Oh okay.
      V: Oka:y? 'Cause I-I usually go to bed early.                (V 123)
```

V's initial *if*-clause encodes a situation that might occur as a result of the situation expressed in B's previous announcement. The expected time of B's arrival leads to a problematic contingency. The *if*-clause presents the problem that might arise based on the plan so far: V may go to bed and thus not be able to let B in the door. This option, which follows from the point reached in the prior talk (B's announcement), is encoded in an initial *if*-clause, which then frames the following clause, the solution to the possible problem.

The interactional work of this initial *if*-clause can be gleaned from an understanding of the potentially delicate situation in which V finds herself in this span of talk. She is handling an eventuality related to B's visit. Notice that B's announcement that he will arrive at midnight is responded to with dismay: *Shyoo!*. Next, in an initial *if*-clause, V presents the hypothetical option that she may go to bed early. But in her next turn, she makes it clear that she *usually* does go to bed early. Thus, the *if*-clause which presents an option is serving as a vehicle for introducing problematic news in a mitigated way, the news being that the late hour of arrival is, in fact, an inconvenience.

Earlier in the same conversation between V and B, we find two other examples of the interactive use of *if*-clauses of option as a means of dealing with interpersonally delicate sequences involving the hesitancy of one participant. In example 10, as in example 9, V is displaying a sense of being imposed upon by aspects of the planned visit. Both V and B use *if*-clauses in the exchanges that center on V's hesitations. Where this excerpt begins, B has just reported that he will be arriving that evening rather than the next day.

Initial adverbial clauses

(10)
```
                                    (just)
   1   B:  Is that okay? (.) I c⌈an (either) stay with you or
   2       with Sco:tt,         ⌊
   3   V:                        ⌊Ye-
   4   V:  No that's fine, stay he:re. .hhh U:mm
   5       (.)
   6   B:  I'll probably end up staying with Scott. After-
   7       after a while maybe.
   8       (0.2)
   9   V:  We:ll un-nuh-u:h it's fine. The only thing is,
→ 10       t'just realize, that if I have to study at times:
  11       (0.4) actually I have to study a lot. Just dow-
  12   B:  =Both of you do. I know.=Well I'm (.) down there
  13       (.) not to be part o'you c(hh)uttin into uh
  14   V:  Uh (h)huh,
  15   B:  Uh t(h)o (h)his research, (.) bu:t y'know
  16       (company) an' things like that.
  17   V:  Uh hh⌈huh   (.) An' you have your ca:r. So
  18       that'll make it quite easy.
  20   B:  Yeah
  21   V:  .hhh Oka:y, is there any kind of food you want me
  22       to g(h)et?
  23       (0.9)
→ 24   B:  Ah-ha well if you do:n't want me to co:me Violet.
  25   V:  Wu-⌈of course- I no of course I actually you know=
  26   B:     ⌊hhhh hhh!huh hhh nuh huh huh hh
  27   V:  ⌈what I'm doing, right now, for you, ⌈tomorrow is=
  28   B:  ⌊.hhh                                ⌊hhh
  29   V:  =I'm vacuuming right now.          (V 32-59)
```

Both the initial *if*-clauses in this example present options, and both arise as accounts or interpretations of V's lack of enthusiasm about B's upcoming visit.

Before I discuss the interactional work of these two *if*-clauses, let me point to the evidence, from the participants themselves, that V is seen as having problems with the planned visit. The span of talk reproduced here begins with a direct question by B about whether it is *okay* that he is coming. By posing this question, B displays concern as to whether V approves of the plan. After B's question, at line 1, V does not come in immediately with a clear positive response. In fact, there is a short, but interactionally significant pause after the question.[6] A pause is particularly indicative of trouble in this position, after a question specifically checking on the acceptability of B's proposed plan. B's continuation after the pause is a direct response to the pause. His continuation further displays his sense that V may not like the proposed plan: B offers to stay with a friend instead of with V. Just after B initiates this offer, V does come in with what looks like a positive answer to the original question, but she cuts that off and lets B finish his offer. V declines the offer and reaffirms that it is *fine* for B to stay with her. But B goes on to give an alternate version of the original offer to stay with a friend (line 6), and V again declines and affirms that B's plan is *fine*. V goes on, however, to give an account for her hesitation. By presenting this account, V is validating B's sense that there is a problem. Thus, his earlier interpretation was not mistaken.

Interestingly, B does not seem convinced that V is really communicating a welcome to his visit. V has moved away from the problem of where B will stay to the issue of what food he wants, but B does not respond to V's question. Instead, there is a long pause (line 23), after which B again displays his perception that V has a problem with his upcoming visit.

With all this as evidence that there is some kind of problem recognized by both parties in this sequence, let's see how the *if*-clauses figure in dealing with the problem. The first *if*-clause, at line 10, comes as part of an account by V for why she has been hesitant. The *if*-clause is prefaced with *the only thing is, t'just realize*, which marks what comes next as the cause for V's lack of enthusiasm. Here, V presents the problem, her need to study, as hypothetical. The option presented in the *if*-clause involves the possibility that V will have to *study at times*. She never completes a main clause consequence of the hypothetical option. However, she does restate the content of the conditional clause, this time not as a hypothetical option, but as the real case, *actually I have to study a lot*. Notice that this is a strategy similar to that V uses in example 9 above. V first introduces the information as hypothetical and then states it as a certainty. By using an *if*-clause to introduce the complicating or problematic information, V takes advantage of the backgrounding function associated with initial adverbial clauses. Presenting delicate information first as background seems, then, to be a way of mitigating its impact, bringing it into the conversation through the back door, as it were. V, then, revises her own talk by saying that what was first encoded as hypothetical is *actually* the real case. What we see, then, in the first *if*-clause in this example, is the use of the hypotheticality and backgrounding function of an initial conditional clause as a means of presenting delicate information.

In the second *if*-clause in example 10, we find that, after picking up enough signals that V is not happy about his visit, B draws explicit attention to the interpersonally delicate situation by using a conditional that presents an option, *well if you don't want me to come Violet*. Here, B uses a conditional of option as a way of showing his interpretation of V's previous talk. His conditional clearly displays that he understands V to be feeling negative about his visit; it brings the problematic nature of V's attitude into focus, and at the same time, the hypothetical presentation maintains a polite recognition that this is *just* a possible reading of V's state of mind. Note that B's *if*-clause is not followed by a main clause. The conditional clause alone does the interactional work.

In examples 9 and 10, the initial *if*-clauses presented options that became available at a point in the talk, but that had not been explicitly mentioned before. There is another type of initial *if*-clause that restates an option that has already been presented in the preceding discourse. Ford and Thompson (1986) called these "assuming" conditionals. Rather than introducing a new option, these *if*-clauses select some assertion from the prior discourse and explore the implications of choosing it as an option. In the present data, initial *if*-clauses are also used to restate an option already introduced in the prior talk.

The next two examples, 11 and 12, come from the pre-closing portion of a telephone conversation between two college-aged friends. Making plans for a next meeting characteristically comes before the close of a conversation (Schegloff and Sacks 1973). These excerpts contain several instances of one of the young women using *if*-clauses to propose actions she would like her friend to take. In these cases, A chooses possible options and encodes these options in initial *if*-clauses. She then uses those backgrounded options to present outcomes that she hopes will seem attractive to her interlocutor, B. Thus, she uses *if*-clauses in an interactional strategy of persuasion.

In example 11, A asks B what time B is planning to leave for the city the next day. B responds equivocally, giving three different times. A jumps in after she hears the time at which she is available. At that point, A incorporates the time into an *if*-clause and makes an offer that is contingent on the option restated in the *if*-clause:

(11)
    A: ... So what time y'leaving f'the city,
    B: Oh:: probly abou-t te⌈n-
    A: ⌊((ringing sound))
    B: -ten thirty eleven, or-⌈n-d-ih .hh
                        ⌊Oh   If you wanna leave about eleven,
→   [I'll walk down with [you °cause I have to go to school.
                                               (TG 629–636)

This, then, is a case of an initial *if*-clause used in the information relation of selecting an alternative from the prior discourse. The strategy of encoding the option in an initial *if*-clause is used interactively to make a contingent offer. The fact that A selects an option from B's prior talk gives a sense that the two parties are reaching a decision together.

Somewhat further on in the same sequence, A uses initial *if*-clauses two more times as part of her effort to persuade B to cooperate with the plan to coordinate on going into the city. At this point in the talk, the option of the two women going into the city together has already been a topic of talk.

(12)
                                      (down)
→   A: Maybe if yih come down, I'll take the car (then).
      B: t! We:ll, ud-yihknow I-I don't wanna make any- thing definite. Because I-yihknow I jus:: I jus::t thinkin:g today all day riding on th'trai:ns, hhuh-uh .hh⌈h!
      A: ⌊Well there's nothing else to do. I was thinkin⌈g of taking the car anyway.   .hh
      B: ⌊that I would go into the ss-uh=I would go into the city but I don't know,
→   A: Well if I do ta:ke it, this way if- uh-if-y'know uh:: there's no pa:rking right away, I can give you the car, an' you can look around a little bit.   (TG 682)

Where this excerpt begins, we find the first *if*-clause presenting that option as background for another potentially attractive possi-

Initial adverbial clauses

bility: that A will take her car. The option of A taking her car is, in fact, probably more attractive to her than to the recipient, B, since parking in the city (New York) is a notorious problem. But in any case, the combination of an initial *if*-clause that restates the option of B coming in with A provides a background for what A sees as a positive outcome, that A will take her car.

In the second occurrence of an initial *if*-clause, the offer of taking the car is now used as background for the presentation of another offer: that A will let B use the car once they get to the city. The persuasive use of initial *if*-clauses involves the linking of a potential action (on the part of the recipient or the speaker) with some positively valued outcome, a reward based on a contingent action. The positively valued outcome, presented in the main clause, is a critical component of the interactional use of *if*-clauses in such contingent offers. In fact, the two clauses in these complexes have different subjects: one is the speaker (*I*) the other the recipient (*you*). Thus, the persuasive use of conditionals involves a connection of speaker and recipient through contingent actions.

The span of talk in example 12 actually contains three initial *if*-clauses presenting options; the third one, *if-y'know uh there's no parking right away*, is not working as part of the persuasive conditional complex, but rather simply presents an option that is possible at that point (a contingency that is necessary for the larger persuasive move). Notice that this *if*-clause does not have either the speaker or recipient as subject. The clause presents an impersonal eventuality, not a contingent action tying speaker and recipient.

Examples 11 and 12, then, show how initial *if*-clauses presenting options which create a context for potentially attractive consequences are used interactively in a persuasive interchange.

If-clauses used to present options are not always connected to distinct main clauses. The optionality or hypotheticality expressed in the *if*-clause seems to mark the offer, very overtly, as contingent on the recipient's desire and choice. Here are two such instances from the same sequence cited in examples 11 and 12 above:

(13)
    A: Tch! But if you wanna-uh:m (0.2) come in, an' see.
    B: Tch! I wouldn't know where to look for her(hh) hnhh-hnhh!
                                                          (TG 665)

(14)
```
A:  Well if you want me (to) give you a ring tomorrow morning.
B:  Tch! .hhh Well y-you know, let's, eh- I don't know, I'll see
    (h)may[be I won't even be in,
                                                    (TG 739)
```

B's responses to both of A's turns show that B is interpreting the *if*-clauses as offers. B does not actually refuse the offers, but she provides typical dispreferred responses in the form of accounts for why she may not be able to accept the offers. It is significant that A's *if*-clauses come in a context where B has shown herself to be hesitant about accepting A's offer. The optionality conveyed through the *if*-clause format seems to be chosen in sequences involving interactionally problematic hesitancy on the part of one of the participants.

Another way that initial *if*-clauses are used to present options or possibilities involves the presentation of information that is to be treated as shared. In such cases, although the information may not appear in the prior discourse, the speaker is asking the listeners to take it as given. Simply by using the information pattern of an initial *if*-clause, the speaker is asking the listener to understand the situation as a possibility. These cases involve the use of initial *if*-clauses to present a basis for reasoning.

The excerpt in example 15 is a continuation of the talk about the participants in the fight at the racetrack (see example 4 above). Although the information presented in the initial *if*-clause (at the arrow) does not appear in the prior discourse, G uses the initial *if*-clause to state the basis for his reasoning, the content of the clause being presented as, at least temporarily, given or shared.

(15)
```
                (3.7)
     G:  'N Keegans aren't (always) very big are they?
                (0.4)
     M:  No. They're a⌈ll thin.
     C:              ⌊they're not they're not to⌈o bi:g but-
→    G:                                         ⌊('T's right) if
         they're all Keegans like the ones around Greensprings, they're
         all kind of ⌈bout five five, five six.
     M:             ⌊They're all from around
         Greensprings.                                  (AD 14.15)
```

Example 16, below, is another example of an *if*-clause presenting information to be treated as shared and used as a basis for reasoning.

(16)
```
        C: Is that what your mom thought was unnecessary °⎡(now)
        V:                                               ⎣No
           she: thinks that the whole thing's unnecessary.
           C⎡ause he-
        C:  ⎣(Oh yeah)
        V: he's in so much pain, that it seems like he's never gonna walk
           again. An' she's saying his leg's gonna be an inch shor:ter?
        K: °teh Oh shit.⎡(  )
        V:              ⎣This is what my mom's saying.
           (0.4)
        V: Because they took it out-, this is her, the doctor didn't say his
           leg's gonna be an inch shorter. She's saying it. .hh an' that it's
           unnecessary:, an' there's no re:ason for it, an' on an' on an'
           on an' on.
→       K: (Well) if your mom's so wrong about so much stuff, why
           would she b-all of a sudden be an expert on that.    (K 132)
```

The basis of reasoning is not information already shared through the prior context; rather, the information is being presented as reasonable to assume to be shared precisely through the use of the format of an initial *if*-clause. In this conversation, K has been complaining about the way V lets her mother upset her. V is repeating what her mother has been saying about her father's knee operation. Her mother's reaction to the operation has caused V a good deal of concern, and this is what K is objecting to. K brings in a fact that is presumably understood by V and uses that fact as a basis for questioning the validity of V's mother's thinking. Such uses of initial *if*-clauses state options as given or assumed in a way that is similar to cases in which the information actually has appeared in the prior talk.

There is a final environment in which the use of initial *if*-clauses presenting options has interactional significance. In the following cases, turns are cut off in order for initial *if*-clauses to be inserted. As outlined in 1.1, points of grammatical completion in conversation are the points at which listeners have the opportunity to become speakers, that is, at which turn transfer may take place. In extended turns, such as stories or explanations, points of grammatical completion are locations for recipients to display that they are monitoring the on-going talk (through what have often been termed "back channel" turns: *mm hm, yeah,* etc.) In the cases to be discussed here, the contingencies expressed in the *if*-clauses need to be introduced before a point of possible completion is reached. Ordering an adverbial clause before its main clause insures that no point of possible completion will be reached before the entire clause complex is delivered. In these contexts, completion of the main clauses without the introduction of the conditional clause might lead to unfavorable interactional consequences. In the cases to be discussed here, there seems to be a tolerance of disfluencies in the service of achieving initial position for interactionally consequential contingencies.

There are two cases in the data in which the stream of talk is interrupted to add a contingency. Both these cases involve reported speech. It seems that the first priority is to mark the speech as reported, through some reportative framing device. After the reportative frame is established, the actual content of the reported speech is packaged. In both of the following cases the packaging of the reported speech does not flow smoothly from the reportative frame, and the disjunction is marked by some disfluency, a cut-off and pause in the first case, and a sound stretch in the second.

The first case is part of a lengthy explanation of V's father's knee operation. Here V presents the options that the doctors proposed for dealing with the knee problem:

(17)
```
      V:  This side of the cartilage, wa- b-being worn (it-)
          ga-gone. in his kne⎡e, an' it was swelling .hh
      C:                     ⎣Mm
      V:  So the doctors said, that they would- (0.3)
  →       IF he: (0.5) didn't wanna keep being active, an' do sports n'
          things, right now, at his age, an' with the bad condition of his
          knee, they normally put in a plastic knee.
              (0.2)                                                    (K 76)
```

In this example, the reportative frame has been developed up to the verb *would*, which is, then, cut off and followed by a pause, probably signaling packaging problems. The *If* that follows is delivered with higher amplitude, and the pronoun *he* has a sound stretch. The amplitude and sound stretch introduce a strong set of contingencies encoded in an *if*-clause structure. V's father, the one whose knee is in question, is very active in sports, so the contingency that one should not want to be active in sports will not be met. The adverb *normally* in the clause that follows the extended condition marks the return to the meaning expressed by *would* in the reported speech just prior to the conditional. This *would* was intended not as the past tense of *will*, as could be the case in the reporting of past speech, but rather as the *would* used to report normal or customary activities in the past. As can be seen in the talk that follows the portion shown above, the normal surgical procedure is not what is used on V's father.

(18)
```
    V: A whol:e kn⌈ee replacement.
    C:           ⌊If he didn't wanna be active but
       ⌈since he wa:nted to be active,
    V: ⌊If he didn't want to.
    V: Since my dad wants to ⌈con
    C:                       ⌊I can imagine your dad saying
       no no, that's alright, I won't be active.
    V: Oh ⌈no no no. He wouldn't do that.=
    K:    ⌊Huh huh huh
    V: =cause he wants to continue ski:ing⌈n' stuff.
    C:                                    ⌊right
    V: So they said okay in that case, (0.2) we will cut a we:dge out,
       (0.5) and straighten the leg.                          (K 76)
```

The presentation of the procedure not used, and the contingencies associated with it are meant to project the contrast that V delivers when she describes the procedure ultimately used. The words *would* and *normally* as well as the amplified delivery of the *If* all foreshadow the upcoming contrast.[7] If the strong contingency were not introduced in the initial *if*-clause, V would come to the end of a unit of talk with the chance of being misunderstood. That is, if V said, "So the doctors said they would put in a plastic knee," she would reach the end of a main clause before the contingency was introduced. C might, then, hear that the normal knee operation is what was done on V's father.

V could, of course, add the contingency in a final *if*-clause, but in delivering the clauses in that order, she would risk prompting a receipt token from C at the end of the main clause. By risking such an uptake, V would also be providing for a possible unwarranted inference with regard to what actually took place in her dad's operation; the inference might then have to be corrected by V in subsequent talk. This could lead to the necessity of adding the *if*-clause in a kind of repair work, clarifying the originally intended meaning. This alternate format would also miss the chance to set up a local organization within V's talk such that the discourse pattern projected an upcoming contrast. The repair that V does in the middle of her turn by inserting the initial *if*-clause marks the local development of her talk as being organized around contrasting options. As can be seen in C's response, she has understood that a contrast is projected by V's talk. Here, then, the format of an initial *if*-clause of option is used even when repair work is necessary to produce it. The interactional motivation for the insertion of an initial *if*-clause is the avoidance of a possible completion point in the turn before the contingency is stated. The option-presenting format projects the further development of the discourse in a contrast.

In the second such case from a different conversation, example 19, V is talking to her brother B about plans for the time he will be spending in Los Angeles, where V lives.[8] The word *whether* is stretched, again a sign of possible problems in packaging the next bit of talk. The *if* that follows is presented parenthetically, with the close in the parentheses and the return to the main talk marked by the repeat of *whether* which comes just after the *if*-clause.

(19)[9]
```
      V: An' also one more thing, Mother wanted to know, whethe::r if
  →      we're going to the desert on the weekend, whether wu-we
         wanted to go to a (.) Halloween party, they were gonna have.
         (.)
      B: Did the:y, huh .hhh                                    (V 77)
```

Here the consequence of not placing the contingency first would be the reaching of possible completion with the implication that the plan was already set for the two to go to the desert.

In fact, plan-making and available time seem to be issues in this conversation. In the fragment below, a bit later in the talk, in response to the mother's question as delivered through V, B hedges on whether he will have time for visiting his parents (first

Initial adverbial clauses 55

arrow). We can see that V is aware that protecting B's schedule is an issue (beginning at the second arrow):

(20)
```
         B:  Uh she-she called, I've gotta call her (in a minute now).
         V:  Oh that's what she called about. I think.
         B:  Oh okay.=
         V:  But we can call her, when you get here.=
    →    B:  Yeah. Well there might not be (.) well (.) it all depends on
             what's going on ( ) the weekend.
                 (0.4)
         B:  In Los Angeles. hh huh huh ⌈huh
         V:                              ⌊Uh hu:h ⌈So you're or-=
         B:                                       ⌊hhh hhh
         V:  =she said is he coming for vacation? or for um (0.4) tsk! .hhh
             work. An' I said I:: do::n kno::w.
         B:  Violeta:!
         V:  I said ⌈both.
         B:         ⌊You're a lot of ba:ckup. Aren't you. For me.
    →    V:  (Uh know), I said- no I said both. It's both.
                 (0.4)
         V:  °Both. See? I defended you.                              (V 92)
```

In the context of the need to *defend* B, presumably from his parents' knowing too much about his private life and plans, the need to carefully manage the contingency of whether V and B were even going to go out to the desert to visit the parents is well-motivated. V's method of presentation in example 19 assures that B does not feel that plans have already been made for his time: she places the salient contingency, *if we're going to the desert on the weekend*, before the main clause, thus avoiding coming to a point of grammatical completion with a potential for misunderstanding.

Examples 17 and 19, illustrate an interactional motivation for using initial position for the presentation of contingencies. The need to avoid possible completion points before the presentation of an interactionally consequential contingency is strong enough that disfluencies are tolerated in the service of achieving initial position for such information. In addition to achieving shifts in the flow of information, then, initial position, and here the option-presenting information format, seem to be favored when there is a potential for misunderstanding if the final placement pattern were used.

In this section, in addition to describing the information patterns whereby initial conditionals present options in the development of talk, I have shown some of the interactional work that can be achieved through the presentation of options. Conditionals presenting options may be used in persuasion, to present offers, and to deliver delicate information in a softened, backgrounded manner.[10] I have also suggested that another motivation for using an initial *if*-clause in an option-presenting format comes from the turn-taking system. Initial placement helps a speaker avoid the potential interactional consequences of final placement: possible loss of the floor before a crucial contingency is expressed.[11]

3.2.3 Introducing the opposite: contrast

Another way in which an initial adverbial clause can relate to what precedes it, and produce a frame for what follows, is through contrast.[12] Initial adverbial clauses of contrast may present an assertion that is the opposite of, or is an option competing with, some assertion or set of assertions from the prior discourse. In this sense, the contrast strategy may be best viewed as a subcategory of the option strategy. It may, in fact, be true that there is some contrast implicit in each presentation of an option, i.e., there is another option unstated, but assumed.

In the following example, M is commenting on the fight that took place at the races the night before the conversation. The man referred to is the driver who started the fight:

(21)
→ M: But yihknow eh- uh-he made his first mistake number one by messin' with Keegan, because the pits'r fulla Keegans, an' when there isn't a Keegan there, there's a Franks.

(AD 12.5)

In this example, an initial *when*-clause presents a contrast with the preceding material. The generalization that the pits are full of Keegans has an exception. The exception is presented in the initial *when*-clause, which is built through a simple negation of the prior material. The initial *when*-clause basically says that, when the previous assertion does not hold, another assertion does. Because Franks are related to Keegans, the effect is the same.

Example 22, below, is another example of an initial adverbial clause presenting a contrast with what precedes it. In this instance, B asks if A ever sees a mutual acquaintance of theirs. A answers negatively but then adds a contrasting exception:

(22)
    A: Mmm
    B: So,
    A: (.hhh)
    B: °That's too bad,
    A: hhhh
       (0.5)
    B: °(So anyway) .hh Hey do you see v- (0.3) fat ol' Vivian anymore?
→ A: No, hardly. An' if we do:, y'know, I just say hello quick'n, .hh y'know, just pass each other in the hall.   (TG 363)

In this case, as in most instances of this function, an initial *if*-clause introduces the contrast. Note that as in example 21 the effect of the contrasting situation is still the same. However, there is an additional interactional motivation for the contrast in example 22. The motivation involves the general tendency for interactants to orient toward agreement (Sacks 1987). A's presentation of an exception is also a vehicle for mitigating a dispreferred response.

Looking more closely at what is taking place in the interaction in example 22, we see that B has just finished reporting on some events in her life, and that topic has closed with the final assessment, *That's too bad*. There is a pause, and then B tries a new line of talk about a mutual acquaintance. B's turn offers a new topic, so the initial *No* in A's response, though presumably dealing honestly with the information asked for in the question, is not picking up on the topic. This makes it a dispreferred response to the topic proffer. Thus, the *hardly* followed by the contrasting *if*-clause *if we do* form steps in the mitigation of a dispreferred response.

Contrasts may also be presented by pairs of initial adverbial clauses. In such cases, the first initial adverbial clause introduces one option, and the second introduces a contrasting option. These cases, in particular, seem to indicate that the contrast strategy is a subcategory of the option-presenting strategy.

In the following example, R is talking about an outline for a

TV script that he has submitted to the producer of a show. He has not heard whether the outline was favorably received or not:

(23)
```
         R: But also I'd like to (.) ya know, get started tryin' to write a
            script out of °it just in case to:o=
         A: =.hhh well uhm:: (0.4) yeah (well) think of other outlines
            too.=
    →    R: =Yeah (.) well .hhh if they take this o:ne, (0.2) then (.)
    →       definitely other outlines.='N i⌈f they don't =
         A:                               ⌊Uh hun
         R: =take this one the:n (0.2) may:be other outlines. I have to
            deci:de.                                              (AR 152)
```

At the arrows, R presents two options, the second contrasting with the first. Notice that R's contrasting pair of *if*-clauses also perform standard interactional work in relation to preference structure. R presents the first *if*-clause as an agreement with A's prior turn. In this manner, R delays presenting the other half of the contrasting pair, the part that does not agree with A's suggestion.

Another of these contrast pairs comes up a few lines later in the same conversation. This time, the consequent of the second *if*-clause, the contrasting option, is not completed – the opposite of *I'm home free* is predictable enough that it need not be stated:

(24)
```
         A: °Yeah of course they might sa:y (0.2) this is go:od,
            (0.5)
         A: Do ya have another one.=
    →    R: =.hhh If they say tha:t, (0.2) the:n (.) I'm home free.
            (0.4)
         R: Then I'm happy.
         A: Yeah,
    →    R: If they s:ay, I'm sorry this is so:: ba:d, (.) I don't know what
            the f-⌈(0.2) wha:t (was in your head)
         A:     ⌊Whh .hhh heh ha ha                                (AR 159)
```

Note that in example 24, as in 23, the contrasting pair format achieves a delay in the delivery of the less aligned, more disagreeing portion of R's response to A.

In another case (discussed earlier in section 3.2.2) a contrast pair is created across speakers. In this example, the first part of the opposition is encoded in an *if*-clause and the second in a *since*-clause.

(25)
```
        V: This side of the cartilage, wa- b-being worn (it-) ga-gone. in
           his kne⌈e, an' it was swelling .hh
        C:      ⌊Mm
        V: So the doctors said, that they would- (0.3)
→          IF he: (0.5) didn't wanna keep being active, an' do sports n'
           things, right now, at his age, an' with the bad condition of his
           knee, they normally put in a plastic knee.
              (0.2)
        V: A whol:e kn⌈ee replacement.
→       C:           ⌊If he didn't wanna be active but
→          ⌈since he wa:nted to be active,
        V: ⌊If he didn't want to.
        V: Since my dad wants to⌈con
        C:                      ⌊I can imagine your dad saying
           no no, that's alright, I won't be active.
        V: Oh ⌈no no no. He wouldn't do that.=
        K:   ⌊Huh huh huh
        V: =cause he wants to continue ski:ing⌈n' stuff.
        C:                                    ⌊right
        V: So they said okay in that case, (0.2) we will cut a we:dge out,
           (0.5) and straighten the leg.                              (K 76)
```

In this example, V sets up the first side of the contrast, and C, in a check of understanding, introduces the second half of the opposition. The contingency introduced in V's extended conditional clause is one that C understands to be unmet in the case of V's father. C repeats the contingency and adds the opposing assertion, *but since he wa:nted to be active*, displaying her understanding that the first option was not the one chosen. Note the contrastive stress on *wa:nted*.

To summarize the discussion thus far, contrasts may appear as simple opposites, competing options with reference to some prior assertion, or they may form parts of contrast pairs which, essentially, are spans of talk exploring two options. Ford and Thompson (1986) found cases in which more than two options were presented through such a strategy, but, in this corpus, such oppositions only occurred in pairs.

Another way in which adverbial clauses of contrast may be used interactionally can be seen in example 27 below. Here, C uses an adverbial clause contrast to shift away from a shared line of talk that has been prevailing for quite some time in the conversation. Many transcript pages prior to this utterance, C introduced the question of where he could get a special spring for a car he owns, as shown in example 26:

(26)
    C: He:y,=. Where can I get a::, uh 'member the old twenty three Model T spring,
        (0.5)
    C: Backspring 't came up like that,
        .
        .
        .
    C: Dju know what I'm ⌈talking about,
    M: ⌊Ye:h I think I know what you mean,
    C: Where can I get one.   (AD 22.9–17)

This question touches off several other topics of talk about people who work on, or own, special old cars.

In example 27, below, C tries to change the direction of talk with a series of initial *if*-clauses of contrast (at the arrows), which create shifts from the prior talk and frame a new direction for the talk to follow.

(27)
    C: Well I- see I got my T bucket started-Well
        I ⌈didn't get it started I got it- I'm ta:lkin'=
    G: ⌊((Clears throat))
    C: =about it now I'm, tryin' to get things lined up for it.
        (1.2)
    M: Te⌈e?
    C: ⌊You know what you know the kinda spring I'm talkin' about.
        (0.3)
    C: Th'muh-the o⌈ld model tee-
    M: ⌊Yah they're They're
    C: Yea⌈h.
    M: ⌊They're a hi:gh arch spr⌈ing.
    C: ⌊High arch spring.
    G: ⌈Oh: just across the back end?
    C: ⌊Any-any high arch.

Initial adverbial clauses

```
        C:  °Yeh.
        C:  ⎡Yeh but-
        G:  ⎣Well see (uh my ex) father'n law down'n Port Clint has one
                that's (got) started. He's, got the engine (innit) 'n everything.
                (0.5)
        G:  'N he's got- a spring that comes, (0.7) way up, all-from one
                wheel t'the other.
        C:  Yeah, 't's right,
        G:  Big hi:gh an' this is a twu: I think it's a twenty seven, 'r::
                ⎡twenty eight,
    →   C:  ⎣We:ll anyways if I can't get it- I mean
    →       I'm just lookin' for somethin. If ehy if it's substitute,
                {intervening talk from another conversation}
        G:  But- Uh: hh
    →   C:  =If I can' get that, I'll just have to go, to a lower
                spring. ⎡( )
        M:         ⎣You can get'em ma:de.                    (AD 31.4)
```

After a lengthy discussion of getting an original spring, C moves the talk away from the need to find the exact spring he had in mind. Even though G seems willing to continue the discussion of options for finding an original spring, C attempts to draw that line of talk to an end with *Well anyways* and then the first *if*-clause of contrast, *if I can't get it-* After his series of initial *if*-clauses of contrast, C succeeds in directing the line of talk to a discussion of having a spring made rather than finding an original one. So, in addition to representing a contrast in information, the initial *if*-clause is part of a strategy whereby one party in the conversation attempts to move the talk in another direction (as did a time shift *when*-clause in example 7, above).

So, as with initial adverbial clauses encoding options, those which form contrasts also have strategic interactional functions in shifting the direction of talk or mitigating dispreferred responses.

3.3 Summary

What has been presented in sections 3.2.1 through 3.2.3 is an outline of how initial adverbial clauses form information management patterns and do interactional work in conversational discourse. Initial adverbial clauses tie back to previous discourse in specific ways. Temporal clauses introduce time frames and encode shifts in time: shifts from a general or non-specific time to

Table 4. *Types of initial adverbial clauses*

Function	Time frame	Option	Contrast	Total
Clause type				
Temporal	22		1	23
Conditional		24	10	34
Causal			1	1
Concessive			1	1
Totals	22	24	13	59

Numbers include adverbial clauses without main clauses that function similarly to initial adverbial clauses.

a more specific time reference, ordered shifts in the presentation of sequenced events, and shifts from specific to generic or non-specific time reference. Conditional clauses are used to present options that follow from points reached in prior discourse, to restate options that have appeared in prior discourse, or to present possibilities as at least temporarily shared. In a related strategy, initial adverbial clauses, primarily conditionals, may present contrasts to material presented in prior talk. In all these cases, initial adverbial clauses form pivotal points in the development of talk and present explicit background for material that follows.

Table 4 above, summarizes the discourse patterns created by initial adverbial clauses, and the number of occurrences of those types in the corpus.

In conjunction with the discussion of initial adverbial clauses in terms of information patterns, I have presented some of the ways that conversationalists use initial adverbial clauses in more interactionally significant ways. In addition to being analyzable in terms of information patterns, initial adverbial clauses can be understood with respect to their interactional potential. They are invoked in attempts to shift the direction of talk, to close down others' lengthy turns, to make or tone down offers, to persuade, or to mitigate the force of a dispreferred response. I have supported my interpretations of the interactional functions of initial adverbial clauses with detailed evidence from the conversational context of the cases cited.

4

Final versus initial adverbial clauses in continuous intonation

4.1 Overview

Unlike initial adverbial clauses in these data, which always end in continuing intonation, when adverbial clauses appear after their associated modified material, they may be connected to that material across continuing or ending intonation. There are 135 final adverbial clauses, making up 66% of the adverbial clauses in the data. Of these final adverbial clauses, 40 (30%) are temporal (*when, while, before, after* etc.), 18 (13%) are conditional (*if*), 75 (56%) are causal (*because, 'cause*), and 2 (1%) are concessive (*although, even though*).

Eighty (59%) of the final adverbial clauses occur after continuing intonation, while 55 (41%) link back to utterances ending in final falling intonation.

The distinction between continuing and final intonation reflects speakers' decisions to signal that an utterance is not yet completed (continuing intonation), or that an utterance is possibly complete (final intonation). Schiffrin (1987) used this intonation distinction to separate intra-utterance conjunction from inter-utterance conjunction in her analysis of interview data. By distinguishing intra- from inter-utterance intonation patterns, one can describe grammatical connections that occur as parts of intonationally coherent units, and compare these connections to grammatical connections that occur across final intonation boundaries.

In the present chapter I describe the use of adverbial clauses following continuing intonation. In the next chapter, I look at adverbial clauses added to utterances that have been presented as intonationally complete. Final adverbial clauses after continuing

Table 5. *Final adverbial clauses*

Temporal	Conditional	Causal	Concessive	Total
40 (30%)	18 (13%)	75 (56%)	2 (1%)	135 (100%)

Table 6. *Intonation preceding final adverbial clauses*

After continuing intonation	After final intonation	Total
80 (59%)	55 (41%)	135 (100%)

Table 7. *Adverbial clauses by position and intonation*

	Temporal	Conditional	Causal	Total
Initial	21	26	—	47
Final continuing[a]	33 (41%)	12 (15%)	35 (44%)	80 (100%)
Final ending	7	6	40	53
Total	61	44	75	180[1]

[a] Intonation on preceding clause.

intonation are of three types in my corpus: temporal, conditional, and causal. Of these three, only temporal and conditional clauses appear both before and after their main clauses, while causal clauses appear only *after* the material they modify. Thus, causal clauses in these conversations do not participate in the functional dichotomy of initial versus final positioning. Section 4.3 presents the distribution of temporal and conditional clauses, outlining their functions and comparing these with the work of the same sorts of clauses when they appear initially (as described in chapter 3). Patterns of causal clause usage are described in section 4.4, where I argue that such clauses are fundamentally different from temporals and conditionals in their use in these conversations.

Before discussing the occurrences of final adverbial clauses in the corpus, I would like to review briefly the notion of "theme" in discourse connection. Such a review is relevant to an account of cases in which initial position is not selected for adverbial clause placement.

4.2 Initial position and discourse connection

As was discussed in chapter 3, an adverbial clause in initial position ties the present utterance back to the previous discourse and introduces or frames the discourse that follows. This tying back and framing function is not peculiar to initial adverbial clauses. In fact, there is a generally recognized strategy in English whereby the initial constituent of a clause, or the initial clause in a clause complex, serves as a pivotal point in the development of discourse. In textually oriented analyses, the initial unit in a sentence which serves this pivotal function is commonly referred to as *theme* (Mathesius 1942, Halliday 1967, Fries 1983). Paraphrasing Daneš (1974), Brown and Yule (1983) characterize the functions of theme as the following:

   (i) connecting back and linking in to the previous discourse, maintaining a coherent point of view
   (ii) serving as a point of departure for the further development of the discourse.   (Brown and Yule 1983:133)

In any discussion of theme in English, there is inevitably some reference to the fact that a common thematic element in English clauses is the subject. This stands to reason, since the subject noun phrase regularly encodes the entity which is being talked about in the discourse, and thus the entity around which the discourse is organized and through which the clauses in the discourse are connected (Brown and Yule 1983:131–138).

The placement of an adverbial clause before a main clause is only one option for the creation of links between clauses in discourse. In many instances of adverbial clauses in the present corpus, the main clause clearly connects back to the prior discourse, and no manipulation of temporal or conditional frame is employed in the organization of the discourse. Even when some form of contrast or qualification is made, it may also be made through contrastive elements in a main clause rather than through the introduction of an initial adverbial clause. Thus, in the following example (an example that I return to several times in the chapter), the discourse is organized around changes in the actions of the students: they laugh, they nod, they raise their hands, and they walk out of class. An initial adverbial clause is used to create only the final shift in the students' actions, moving them temporally and spatially out of class.

(1)
```
         B: I-ah- y-yihknow this gu:y has not done anything yet that I
            understa:nd. An' no one eh- no one else in the class under-
    →       stands him either. .hhh We all sit there an' .hh we laugh at his
            jokes, hhh
         A: =Ye:h ⌈I know
    →    B:       ⌊.hhh an' we no:d, when he wants us to say
            yes? (h)e ⌈n .hhh
         A:         ⌊Yeah,=
    →    B: =We raise our ha:nds, when he wants to take a
            po:ll? 'n ⌈: :
         A:         ⌊Ye:h.
    →    B: .hh Yihknow but when we walk out of the cla:ss,
         A: =Nobody knows what ⌈wen' on.]
         B:                    ⌊Wid- .hh h
         B: Li(hh)ke wu—.hh Did you n- Did you know what he was
            talking about? Did you know what structural paralysis was?
                                                              (TG 247)
```

The clauses presenting the second two actions of the students (at the second and third arrows) are connected through the repetition of the subject in initial position. The change in action is simply presented through the different verbs, and no special nonsubject, initial element is used. The contrast between each action segment is made through the different actions of the students, not through the situations which prompt the actions. So, while the first two *when*-clauses represent changes, the discourse has not been organized through those changes, but rather through the changes in the students' responses to the situations. The third *when*-clause, on the other hand, does achieve a realignment in the discourse. A new frame is created through the temporal/spatial shift, *when we walk out of the cla:ss*. Note again that the initial *when*-clause also involves the introduction of a crucial point in the story. The story was originally introduced with the statement that the teacher *has not done anything yet that I understand*. Thus, the contrast between the regimented responses in class and the true level of understanding admitted to out of class represents the point of the story. The two final *when*-clauses, then, are not used as points of departure in the organization of the talk; that work is done by the reports of the changes in the students actions. Initial position is, however, drawn upon at a critical shift point in the story.

There is nothing remarkable about the pattern of subject followed by verb followed by adverbial element; this is a typical English sentence pattern. The fact that each new mention of the same topic entity in initial position may present a new action or event in relation to that entity is not remarkable either. Linear connections in discourse are regularly made through main clauses with coreferential subjects, and these connections may also involve contrasts such as the shifts in the actions of the students in example 1 above.

Considering that initial position in a clause is the location for discourse connection, and that such connections are commonly made by non-adverbial elements such as noun phrases, one can expect to find many clause complexes in which discourse continuity is achieved without the intervention of an initial adverbial clause. The initial placement option for adverbial clauses provides a resource for the connection of clauses in discourse, but an adverbial clause may also appear after its associated main clause, completing a unit of information without serving any pivotal discourse organizational function. When placed after a main clause but in continuing intonation, an adverbial clause presents new information elaborating the main clause rather than providing a pivotal frame for what follows.

4.3 Final temporal and conditional clauses

Temporal and conditional clauses, whether they occur initially or finally, serve to locate events or actions in time or to qualify the interpretation of events or actions. As demonstrated in chapter 3, initial temporal and conditional clauses form pivotal organizational links in the development of discourse, pivotal points that may also correspond to interactional connections and discontinuities. While final temporal and conditional clauses qualify, locate and complete the meaning of utterances, they do not create discourse-level links or shifts. That this is the case in monologue data has been variously shown in the work of Chafe (1984), Ford and Thompson (1986), and Ramsay (1987).

In this section, after showing the ways final temporal and conditional clauses occur in this conversational database, I will offer quantified evidence that final position is the default location for adverbial clauses, with initial position used primarily in sections of talk where one party has particular need for managing the flow of information. Initial temporal and conditional clauses are favored in sections of talk where a single party has an extended hold on the floor. Final adverbial clauses, clauses not associated with discourse-organizational functions, are favored in turn-by-turn talk.

4.3.1 Temporal clauses and information completion

As shown in chapter 3, temporal adverbial clauses may create links in the presentation of sequenced events. The following fragment, from an extended turn by V, shows how the talk is organized through two initial *when*-clauses involving temporal shifts.

(2)
→
→
    V: There was no confusion. An' I was calm with it, 'n then when- when your mom said that, I was frustrated. Like oh that's ridiculous, but then when I talked to my mom, an'she was all hysterical, then I started getting hysterical. (K 198–99)

When a temporal clause occurs finally, the talk is not being organized around a temporal shift, and the adverbial clause merely completes or narrows the meaning of the prior clause. In the following example, H is describing some of the characters in a movie. N shows particular interest at one point in the story and H teases N about this.

(3)
    H: Oh an' then the one that's bigoted, .hhh she's married to this guy who's, (.) really quiet an' inhibited an ⌈it turns out=
    N: ⌊Uh hu:h,
    H: =like she's frigid an' everything an' she

```
       ⎡covers up for it by being yihknow all-khhhhhh!=
   N:  ⎣A::ll ri::ght,
   H: =huh ⎡huh hheh hh hhhhhhhhhhinh huh ehh=
   N:     ⎣So basically, n-hn-hn
→  H: =You got all excited, when I said the frigid
       p⎡art hu:h.
   N:   ⎣Yeah. I mean she dese:rves it.          (HG 12.20)
```

H's talk has moved back and forth between telling the story and introducing and describing the characters. In the portion of the talk excerpted here H is describing a character. At the arrow, H moves out of the movie-telling mode to comment on N's reaction to *the frigid part*. This comment is not presented as part of the rhetorical development that H was involved in up to that point. The switch from the character description to the teasing aside is marked by the use of the second person pronoun *you*. This signals that H's utterance is about her addressee, N, rather than about any character in the movie. There is a shift here from the movie frame to the present interaction. However, the shift is marked by a pronoun switch, not by an initial adverbial clause. The *when*-clause in this example is not creating a shift in the development of the discourse; it is merely completing the meaning of the prior clause.

In the next example, a final *while*-clause helps to elaborate and complete the meaning of the phrase it follows, and the phrase it follows is itself in an adverbial relation of purpose to a previous main clause. G is talking about the car of an acquaintance.

(4)
```
   G:  In two weeks, he's taking it t'Florida.
       (1.4)
   G:  He's gonna pull it down there, just to goof around with, while
→      he's down there on vacation.              (AD 33.20)
```

As in example 3, the final temporal clause in example 4 does not form a pivotal point in the organization of the talk; it merely specifies further the temporal and situational frame for the main clause action. Whereas an initial temporal clause works both to locate the main clause event or action in time or space, and to create a discourse orientation, a final temporal clause does only the temporal and spatial location work, without participating in the discourse organization.

A final adverbial clause may encode an elaboration of a specific temporal expression that has appeared in the associated main clause. In fact, certain time expressions seem to require that some explication follow in order for the time expression to be meaningful. The following example is from a conversation about a movie that a group of friends have just seen together. The time expression *already* needs explication. The final *when*-clause locates the reference of *already* by providing another event in the time line of the movie.

(5)
```
    W: What are you talking about. D'ya mean the (.) pe⌈tshop?
    H:                                              ⌊When
       he put on his headlight glasses, out in the (.)
       ⌈wilds?
    C: ⌊Oh ⌈(hhuh- Eh-h)
    W:     │Oh.
    D:     ⌊(Eheh heh heh)
    C: I thought he had them on already,
→      ⌈when they were showing his eye:s.
    J: ⌊(huh hh                                      (AM 19)
```

The *when*-clause in this example is not involved in a shift in the continuity of a stream of events or a logical sequence. In fact, it is the main clause that creates the continuity by referring back to the shared topic of talk, *them*, the *headlight glasses*.

Example 6 below is another case of a final temporal clause completing the meaning of the immediately prior time expression. Here, the meaning of *first time* is specified in the *since*-clause.

(6)
```
    A: I'm so:: ti:red. I j's played ba:sketball t'day, (this is) the first
→      time since I was a freshman in hi:ghschool.       (TG 48)
```

It may be remembered that initial temporal clauses serve as specifications of immediately prior temporal expressions, as in the *then when* pairs in example 2 from this chapter.

(2) (Repeated)
```
    V: There was no confusion. An' I was calm with it, 'n then when-
→      when your mom said that, I was frustrated. Like oh that's
       ridiculous, but then when I talked to my mom, an'she was all
→      hysterical, then I started getting hysterical.   (K 198–199)
```

Final adverbial clauses in continuous intonation

Here, however, the adverbial clauses not only explicate the prior time expression, but also introduce a new piece of the story, thus serving the characteristically discourse-organizational function associated with initial position. In contrast, the final temporal clauses in this corpus can be analyzed as working at the sentence level to complete the meaning of associated main clauses, without creating links or shifts in discourse development.

In addition to the results of a case-by-case analysis, there are two other kinds of support for my claim that the function of final temporal clauses is to elaborate and specify a sentence rather than to serve as pivotal discourse-organizational elements.

Evidence from conversational repair also suggests that some final temporal clauses function more as sub-parts of main clauses than as separate elements at a higher level of discourse. In example 7, the message of the main clause is presented, and then, during the presentation of the time element, some disfluency is evident. B is giving her friend an update on B's grandmother's health.

(7)
      B: so I don't know, I haven:'t yihknow, she wasn't home, by the
→   t-yih know, when I left for school today.   (TG 90)

The disfluency comes after the time element has been partially formulated. What appears to be *by the time* is then replaced with *when*, and the final adverbial is completed. One interpretation of the hesitation and replacement is that the main clause message was formulated with a slot for specification of time, but the exact formulation of that time was done after the delivery of the main clause. This sort of repair never occurs with initial temporal clauses, which function as pivotal points in the development of the discourse, rather than slots to be filled by any one of several appropriate time elements to complete a sentence message.[2]

In example 8, another example of mid-sentence repair, we find what appears to be the beginning of a final *when*-clause replaced by a prepositional phrase.

(8)
      V: So then .hh I was the:re, I was there. I heard it, doctor knew
      what he was talking about, made my dad feel comfortable,
→   said that he's gonna have this same operation, when he's – in

about (0.2) twenty years, cause he had bad knees from
football, n-in highschool.   (K 152)

Again, there is a main clause delivered intact, and then a partial delivery of the time adverbial. The disfluency seems to reflect some problem in computing the doctor's projected age. The replacement of the *when*-clause with a prepositional phrase helps the speaker avoid doing an exact computation (although even the expression of *twenty years* is also preceded by hesitation).

Cases such as those in examples 7 and 8 suggest that final temporal clauses represent completion and specification of main clause verb meaning; as such, they commonly fill final slots associated with verb elaboration. As evidenced from the repairs in these examples, the slots filled by final temporal clauses may alternatively be filled by other temporal clauses or by prepositional phrases that serve the same verb specifying function.

A second kind of evidence that suggests that final temporal clauses alternate with other post-verbal grammatical structures, particularly prepositional phrases, in completing clausal information can be seen in the parallel sentences of a description of the poor instructor (discussed earlier as example 1):

(9)
```
       B: Oh my, my North American Indian class is really, (0.5) tch!
          It's so boring.
             (0.3)
       A: Ye(h)e(h)ah
             (0.2)
       B: I-ah- y-yihknow this gu:y has not done anything yet that I
          understa:nd. An' no one eh- no one else in the class under-
  →       stands him either. .hhh We all sit there an' .hh we laugh at his
          jokes, hhh
       A: =Ye:h ⎡I know
  →    B:       ⎣.hhh an' we no:d, when he wants us to say
          yes? (h)e⎡n .hhh
       A:          ⎣Yeah,=
  →    B: =We raise our ha:nds, when he wants to take a
          po:ll? 'n⎡ ::
       A:          ⎣Ye:h.
       B: .hh Yihknow but when we walk out of the cla:ss,
       A: =Nobody knows what ⎡wen' on.]
       B:                    ⎣Wid- .hh h
```

Final adverbial clauses in continuous intonation 73

> B: Li(hh)ke wu—.hh Did you n- Did you know what he was talking about? Did you know what structural paralysis was?
>
> (TG 247)

At the three arrows, we find habitual classroom events presented in a list and encoded in parallel structures. The parallelism is in the format:

Action	Prompt for action
we laugh	at his jokes
we nod	when he wants us to say yes
we raise our hands	when he wants to take a poll

As mentioned earlier, the connections between utterances in this piece of talk center on shifts in the reactions of the students rather than shifts in what I call the "prompts." Thus, while the discourse could have been developed around contrasting temporal clauses (in the case of the second two arrows), the speaker instead has selected the shifts between the students' actions as the theme or point of departure which connects the three clause complexes into a series.

What is of relevance to the argument that final temporals fill essentially main clause completing functions is the fact that the first presentation of a "prompt for action" is in the form of a prepositional phrase, while the "prompts for action" in the next two sentences are presented as final *when*-clauses.

Example 9, then, involves a list of clearly parallel structures. In each sentence the verb is completed through a final adverbial, either a prepositional phrase or a temporal clause. In none of the sentences is the adverbial phrase operating at the discourse level to achieve a shift or contrast in the continuity of the developing talk. It is not until the students leave the class and the crux of the story is reached that an initial temporal clause becomes a discourse organizational link.

In this section we have seen that final temporal clauses do not represent points of departure in the organization of discourse; instead, they merely complete the information in a sentence. In completing and narrowing the reference of their associated main clauses, temporal clauses may alternate with prepositional phrases in a sentence-final slot.

4.3.2 Conditional clauses and information completion

Initial conditional clauses, like initial temporal clauses, tie back to previous discourse and provide limited frameworks for the interpretation of clauses to follow.

Similar to initial conditionals, final conditionals qualify and limit the interpretation of the main clauses with which they are associated, but, as in the case of final temporal clauses, they do this without forming pivotal points in the organization of the talk.

In the following example, from a conversation between college friends in a dormitory room, the ringing of the phone has interrupted the talk, and M takes the opportunity to announce that he's leaving.

(10)
      (1.4)
  M: Well anyway listen I gotta go, I gotta do a lot of studying.
      (0.3)
  M: Oh an' Hillary said she'd call me, if- she was gonna go t'the library with me.   (SN 697)

Unlike the cases of initial *if*-clauses, which contrast with, assume information from, or choose options from the prior context, this final *if*-clause does not create any kind of link to the discourse prior to the clause complex. The question of whether or not Hillary was going to the library does not figure in any way, overt or assumed, in the prior discourse. Instead, the *if*-clause makes explicit the condition under which Hillary would call and is presented as essential to the meaning of *would call*; that verb alone would not represent the entire intended meaning.

Example 11 below is another case in which a final conditional clause completes the meaning of a sentence rather than organizing the discourse in relation to the preceding context:

(11)
  C: If I can't get that, I'll just have to go, to a lower spring [( )
  M: [You can get'em ma:de.
  G: S'm guys in Bellview bui [It a frame (en it cost em),
  C: [Yeah, for a fortune,
  G: five hundred tw[o hundred   (two hundred)
  M: [I don't think it's all that much to get a spring made, I think theh-the:re used to be a place up in Toledo

Final adverbial clauses in continuous intonation

→ that'd make'em for ya, if you give'm the dimensions you
   <u>w</u>ant,   (AD 31.22)

The *if*-clause at the beginning of this fragment is discussed in terms of its discourse-organizational and interactional functions in chapter 3 (3.2.3); it presents a contrast with what came before. On the other hand, the final *if*-clause at the arrow is not creating a discourse-level link. The question of whether or not the dimensions could be provided is not connected to the prior discourse, but, in fact, becomes a focus in several turns that follow:

(12)
    C: Well, see I don't know any, I wouldn't know what- (0.4) what dimensions t'even <u>start</u> to give'em.
        (0.4)
    C: Wouldn't know what t'hell he'd want.
    G: Go down there'n measure <u>hi:</u>s. .hh
                                                                    (AD 31.26)

There are, however, contexts where the information content of a final *if*-clause can be viewed as contrasting with some aspect of the discourse prior to the clause complex. But in these contexts it is always the case that the main clause is also presenting a contrast with the prior discourse. In such cases the contrast between utterances is being achieved through the main clause, with the conditional clause reinforcing, but not specifically delivering, the contrast; that is, the discourse is being organized through the contrast in the main clause.

In the following example, G has been teasing his wife K about being dumb, after an incident between them that he feels demonstrates that she is dumb.

(13)
    G: <u>You</u> dumb she⎡ck.
    R: ⎣e:gh.
    G: ((sniff))
    K: <u>Oh:</u> (
    G: ⎡Gary)
                            ⎣M-   One good thing about bein' du:mb,
        (0.8)
    G: <u>You</u> show it very obv⎡i o u s   ⎡ly.
    C: ⎣Mm-mmhhh⎣ mmm
    K: ⎡Ehhhhhhhhhh
                                       ⎣eh-heh-he̅h-<u>heh</u>-

```
            heh-heh!  .hhh
       C:   °hhnh!
       K:   °uh-nh!
       ( )  °hh hn-hn .hh ⎡hn
       G:                 ⎣Ain't no sense in bein' dumb,
  →         if you can't show it once in awhile.         (AD 6.11)
```

Note the parallel presentation of content in G's two utterances: first a clause about being dumb and then one about how it is shown. The final *if*-clause contrasts with the content of the prior discourse, *you show it* . . . versus *if you can't show it*. However, the discourse is developed around the contrast between *One good thing about bein' dumb* and *Ain't no sense in bein' dumb*. The contrast is clear from the negation as well as the stress on the verb in the main clause of the conditional clause complex. Givón (1984:324–329) has suggested an association between negation and presupposed propositions, and thus the use of negation in itself is likely to imply contrast with prior discourse or knowledge. So, while initial conditional clauses may be used to develop a piece of discourse involving contrast, negation of a prior assertion through a main clause is an effective alternative use of contrast as a mode of discourse development, which final conditional clauses can then elaborate on.

Here is a similar discourse development strategy used by the same speaker just a bit further in the conversation. G is ordering a child to put away his friend's toy (segments of an overlapping, unrelated piece of talk by other parties are deleted).

```
(14)
       G:   Whnche go put that up, so that it don't get broke any worse.
  →    G:   Break the whole insides out, if you keep wobblin' that barrel
            around.
               (1.0)
       G:   Go put it u⎡:p.
       C:              ⎣Go on.
       R:   Uh-WHE-E:RE?                                  (AD 6.25)
```

In G's talk, the contrast that is used to connect two utterances is between *so that it don't get broke* . . . and *break the whole insides out* . . . The final conditional clause also expresses a contrast at a strict information level (*put that up* versus *keep wobblin that barrel around*), but the main clause serves as the contrast through which the discourse is connected. The main clause introduces a

Final adverbial clauses in continuous intonation

switch from the negation of *break*, *don't get broke*, to the contrasting affirmative possibility *break the whole insides out*.

In example 14, as in 13, the discourse is organized through the negative/positive polarities in the main clauses, this time moving from negative to positive. As discussed in section 4.2, while initial adverbial clauses can be used to create links in the development of a piece of talk, other common options exist for creating such ties and shifts. In these examples, a switch in the affirmative–negative polarity forms the discourse contrast.

In a final example involving contrast in both main and conditional clauses, an assumed situation, not explicit in the prior discourse, becomes the focus of a contrast. K is reporting on V's mother's anxiety about her husband's knee operation. K and V have just come from the hospital, so the knowledge that V's father is in the hospital is shared by all parties in the conversation (K, V, and C). In this part of K's talk, he describes V's reaction to her mother.

(15)
    K: She was goin'. God do you think they're (.) performing unnecessary surgery on my dad, or some'm like that?
    (0.2)
    K: Just 'cause uh some'm her mom 'ed told 'er.
    (0.5)
→   K: It was really amazing. =(It wz all) you know like Nazi experiments or something. (sd) god he wouldn't be in there, (0.2) if he didn't need it ya know?=
    C: =Yea:h   (K 8–16)

The contrast comes at the arrow, when K uses the negation of the real situation as part of his argument, *he wouldn't be in there, if*... Here, then, we find a segment of talk connected through contrast in a main clause, contrast not to an explicit assertion in the prior talk, but to the shared information that V's father is in the hospital. While the final *if*-clause completes the sentence, it can also be seen as relating to information in the prior discourse, since the question of whether the surgery was *unnecessary* appears several clauses previous to this one. The *if*-clause, if it were initial, would be functioning as selecting and exploring an option from the prior discourse. The development of K's argument would go something like this:

(16)
> It was really amazing. It was all you know like Nazi experiments or something. (sd) god if he didn't need it, he wouldn't be in there.
>
> (hypothetical example)

By placing the *if*-clause initially, there would be a sense that the argument might continue with other consequences of that option. Again, however, as in the previous examples, a contrast created through the main clause is the method of development selected by this speaker.

Sections 4.3.1 and 4.3.2 have illustrated the differences between initial and final temporal and conditional clauses as they function in this conversational corpus. Consistent with the findings of other studies looking at the placement of such clauses, initial temporal and conditional clauses in these data are involved in discourse management work, while such clauses in final position merely complete the main clause meaning.

4.3.3 Temporal and conditional clause position and the turn-taking system

Another type of evidence for the functional division between initial and final placement of temporal and conditional clauses can be found in their distribution with respect to the operation of the conversational turn-taking system. The seminal work on the turn-taking system, Sacks *et al.* (1974), predicted that grammatical embedding to the left would be favored as a means for extending a speaker's hold on the floor. However, left-placed adverbial clauses in this corpus are frequently used when an extended turn has already been established. It is after the normal operation of the turn-taking system has been modified to allow for one party to gain extended hold on the floor, that the information management function of initial placement is most used.

The operation of the turn-taking system places functional demands on interactional language use which are notably absent from monologue language use. Let me review the principles and constraints of the turn-taking system as accounted for by Sacks *et al.*[3] Participants in conversations monitor each other's talk for cues as to when turn-transfer may take place. Speakers can project ahead to upcoming turn-transfer locations based on grammatical

Final adverbial clauses in continuous intonation 79

units such as words, phrases, and clauses. And it is at such transfer points that listeners become speakers and may thereby cooperate in the mutually achieved interaction, displaying their understanding of the prior talk and adding another turn to the sequence underway. The projection of the type of turn one is engaged in is, then, essential to the maintenance of interaction, as it provides one mechanism for coordination and cooperation between parties (see chapter 1, section 1.1.1).

According to Sacks *et al.* (1974), each speaker is initially allotted one sentence, clause or phrase per turn. This means that, unless a speaker has displayed that the discourse unit s/he is producing will require a longer stretch of talk, the other parties in the conversation may treat the present turn as possibly finished at the first point of grammatical completion. This does not mean that there is, necessarily, competition for the floor, but simply that the other participants will treat the first point of grammatical completion as an appropriate location for their responses to the current speaker's talk. However, even though this is a cooperative, rather than competitive, principle, it does create pressure on the current speaker to do special work when s/he intends to produce more than the first grammatical unit that the turn-taking system allocates.

The association between grammatical units and turn units led Sacks *et al.* to predict an interplay between the two systems. Specifically they expected "the prospect of turn transfer at 'first possible relevance place'... [to condition] decisions as between left-embedded and conjoined sentences" (1974:34). The implication for adverbial clause placement is that initial position might be used in conversation as a means for insuring that no point of grammatical completion will be reached before a clause complex is completed. As we saw in the preceding chapter, initial position may be selected, even when some repair work is necessary (3.3.2), when there might be negative consequences if unit completion were signaled before the adverbial clause was produced. What we might expect, then, is a tendency to use initial position in turn-by-turn talk when there is a chance of losing the floor before one's point has been made clearly. In fact, however, the present corpus shows a different pattern.

Discourse produced by speakers involved in especially long

turns, characterized by special rights to the floor, displays a higher frequency of initial temporal and conditional clauses than discourse produced in regular turn-by-turn talk. Interestingly, although this pattern does not bear out expectations based on the principles of the turn-taking system, it is, in fact, best accounted for with reference to the turn-taking system and its provisions for the creation of longer units of talk. It is when such longer stretches of talk have been negotiated that the type of talk is produced in which discourse-management through initial adverbial clauses becomes particularly useful.

The pattern of clause placement in longer segments of talk conforms best to prior findings regarding the discourse-organizational use of adverbial clauses in monologue data. While principles of adverbial clause placement based on monologue data can presuppose that a writer or speaker is able to control the flow of information in a text and thus, will use initial position to manage that flow, no such blanket assumption can be made with conversational data. As noted above, in a conversation, unless special rights of speaking are negotiated, each point of grammatical completion in a person's talk may constitute a point of speaker change. Thus, in ordinary conversation, the turn-taking mechanism works to reduce the length of turns. In order for the discourse-management function of initial adverbial clauses to become useful, a speaker must be engaged in an extended turn, approximating a monologue. In such a turn, a stretch of discourse may be organized through initial adverbial clauses, among other devices. Thus the pressure for shorter turns reduces the opportunity or need to use initial position to control the flow of information or to structure the discourse. It seems, then, that before speakers make use of the discourse-organizational function of initial adverbial clauses, they commonly modify the turn-taking system to allow for an extended unit of talk.

The constraint on the need to use initial position for information-flow management is reflected in the distribution of initial and final temporal and conditional clauses in my data. Most of such clauses in initial position are delivered by persons who have established themselves in primary speakership roles. Primary speakership involves longer turns with more occasions for the type of information management done through initial adverbial clauses. So, while

Final adverbial clauses in continuous intonation 81

there are occasions in normal turn-by-turn talk when speakers use initial adverbial clauses to relate to or orient their talk to the other's prior talk, initial adverbial clauses are more frequent within more "monologue" portions of talk.

The means by which a conversationalist acquires the temporary role of primary speaker, and thereby suspends the operation of the turn-taking system, are well documented in the literature of conversation analysis (Sacks 1974, Sacks, Schegloff and Jefferson 1974, Jefferson 1978, Schegloff 1980). The following example, from my data, is an instance in which the turn-taking system is modified to allow for an extended turn; it also contains an initial *when*-clause. D's long turn presents a sequence of events, and its point of completion is projected pragmatically rather than grammatically. Interim points of grammatical completion are not interpreted as the locations for speaker change. The long turn originates in W's question as to what made the visitors to Nepal the sickest. C and H suggest that you never really know which food you ate caused the effect. D has a different response.

(17)
```
        W:  Well what made you the si:ckest.
                (1.0)
        C:  You could never ⌈identify it.
        D:                  ⌊Mm:.
        H:  =You don't kno:w. Ye:ah
        D:  =No I know. I('d be) pretty sure it was when-
                (0.8)
→       D:  I went to this thing,
                (1.0)
→       D:  When a pe(r)- when a ol:d man reaches seventy seven, they
            have this big ceremony, (i wu)s like his rebir:th er, something.
            An' they do wha- they (.) carry him on his ba:ck, 'n put him
            in a chariot, n' (.) carry him around all the (.) ki:ds drag him
            around through the village, en' stuff (they do all this) the
            n'they have a big fea:st, en they drink they have these bi:g (.)
            jars full of this (.) mm-
                (1.0)
        D:  It's like fermenten:ted wi(n) er- fermented ri:ce. It's like (.)
            they (.) y'know rice.
        W:  Rice Wine?                                       (AM 123)
```

At the first arrow, there is a clause that is grammatically complete, but it suggests an upcoming elaboration of what the *thing* was; thus, more talk is projected. At this point in the conversation, we know that what makes one the *sickest* is at issue, and D makes it clear that he is about to tell what made *him* the sickest. The relatively long pause that follows is evidence that D has achieved primary speakership; none of the other speakers attempts to take a turn. The end of D's story will be identifiable, not simply by grammatical completion, but by the fact that the source of his sickness will be clear. At interim points of grammatical completion, the story recipients will know the story is not yet over. Some speaker change does occur, as when W offers the candidate term *rice wine*; however, the types of responses allowable to the other parties are limited to tokens of acknowledgement or "continuers" (*mm hm*, *yeah*), requests for clarification, and help with terms (such as W's offer). Note that it is in just this extended turn or primary speakership environment that we see background being introduced through an initial *when*-clause (at the second arrow, as discussed in section 3.2.1).

If the temporal and conditional clauses in my data are grouped according to whether or not they are delivered by speakers in primary speakership roles, a pattern emerges. Looking at the first column of Table 8 we see that out of a total of 47 initial adverbial clauses only 13, or 28%, are produced in normal turn-by-turn talk. And looking at the first row we see that, of the temporal and

Table 8. *Temporal and conditional clauses by primary speakership versus turn-by-turn talk*

	Initial	Final	Totals
Turn-by-turn talk	13	24	37
	(35%)	(65%)	(100%)
	(28%)	(54%)	
Primary speaker	34	20	54
	(63%)	(37%)	(100%)
	(72%)	(46%)	
Totals	47	44	91
	(100%)	(100%)	

($X^2 = 10.52$, 1 d.f., $p < .005$)[4]

Final adverbial clauses in continuous intonation 83

conditional clauses produced in turn-by-turn talk, only about a third (35%) are in initial position. In contrast, when the turn-taking system has been modified, and temporal and conditional clauses are produced by parties in primary speakership roles (as in example 22 above), initial position is used more often. In such environments, 34, or 72%, of the initial adverbial clauses are produced. Of the 54 temporal and conditional clauses produced by primary speakers, 63% are in initial position.

Looking back at the fragment in which B complains about the teacher who is so hard to understand, we find another example of an extended turn in which an initial temporal clause performs a discourse-management function. B has been telling A about her school schedule. She now moves from talking about one course to talking about another. Note the pause after *It's so boring* (second line), the subsequent continuer *Yeah* by A, and the second pause. These constitute evidence that B is being treated as the primary speaker and being allowed to produce an extended turn.

(18)
```
      B:  Oh my, my North American Indian class is really, (0.5) tch!
          It's so boring.
          (0.3)
      A:  Ye(h)e(h)ah
          (0.2)
      B:  I-ah- y-yihknow this gu:y has not done anything yet that I
          understa:nd. An' no one eh- no one else in the class under-
          stands him either. .hhh We all sit there an' .hh we laugh at his
          jokes, hhh
      A:  =Ye:h⌈I know
 →    B:        ⌊.hhh an' we no:d, when he wants us to say
          yes? (h)e⌈n .hhh
      A:           ⌊Yeah,=
 →    B:  =We raise our ha:nds, when he want to take a po:ll? 'n⌈::
      A:                                                          ⌊Ye:h.
 →    B:  .hh Yihknow but when we walk out of the cla:ss,
      A:  =Nobody knows what⌈wen' on.⌉
      B:                     ⌊Wid- .hh h
      B:  Li(hh)ke wu—.hh Did you n- Did you know what he was
          talking about? Did you know what structural paralysis was?
                                                            (TG 247)
```

In example 18, there are three *when*-clauses, two final (at the short arrows, discussed in section 4.2 above) and one initial (at the long arrow). As discussed earlier, the adverbial clauses at the first two arrows do not achieve realignments in the discourse, the discourse being organized around the changes in the students' actions rather than by the teacher's actions that prompt the changes. The initial *when*-clause (at the third arrow) does achieve a realignment, with the students now leaving the class. It also introduces the crux of what is being reported: the fact that in reality the students are not following the lecture.

As exemplified in examples 17 and 18, extended turns which exhibit the discourse-management function of initial temporal clauses generally involve the reporting of sequenced events. However, initial conditional clauses also appear in extended turns. In example 19, A is reporting on current events from his life to his friend R. In this section of talk, the subject of talk is the effect of a takeover of the company where A works.

(19)
```
         A:  However with this new company, .hhh they're no:t as:
             generous an: uh Ken Mathis: has asked for a hundred million
             dollar .hhh budget. An: at that time when he got (0.2) the go
             ahead, ABC said okay::, .hhh but with this new company,
             they're (.) kinda fudging now:. .hhh=
→        R:  =Ow::hh=
         A:  =An:da:: so tha- is- is- (0.2) they've already spent millions a
             dollars anyway.
             (0.2)
         A:  Y'know in preproduction. .hhh=
→        R:  =O:hh, I see.=
             (.)
         A:  An: da:: .hhh so:: (.) But the final word won't come (.) until
             the twenty-eighth of October.
             (.)
⟶        A:  So: uh: if its: ye:s, .hhh (.) I could be emplo:yed until
⟶            nineteen-eighty eight, an if it's a no:, (.) then everybody goes
             home that day::. t(hhh hhh hhh)
         R:  Your:: kidding.                                      (YG 147)
```

The fact that A is the primary speaker in this span is evidenced by R's minimal responses at the first two arrows. The information-managing initial *if*-clauses appear at the final two longer arrows. This type of contrasting *if*-clause is discussed in chapter 3, section 3.2.3.

The use of initial position for information flow management

Final adverbial clauses in continuous intonation 85

purposes seems, then, to be most available and useful when the turn-taking system is temporarily modified to allow for an extended turn. So, while at the sentence level one might consider initial and final placement to be equal options, we find that in conversational environments where a speaker has maximum control of the floor (when the turn-taking system is suspended and the speaker is "primary speaker"), initial position is used more frequently. Final position, as has been suggested by prior studies, is the default location for temporal and conditional clauses. When these clauses appear finally, temporal grounding or conditional qualification is provided for an utterance for reasons not related to discourse level information flow management.

4.3.4 Summary: final temporal and conditional clauses

Based on the analyses of final temporal and conditional clauses on a case-by-case basis, as well as evidence from quantified data related to the turn-taking-system, this section has made a case for the non-discourse level functioning of final temporal and conditional clauses. In their contexts, final temporal and conditional clauses serve to complete sentence information, with elements in their associated main clauses creating discourse level linkages. While contrast and shift functions are combined with the qualification and limitation functions of temporal and conditional clauses in initial position, the same types of clauses in final position serve only the qualifying and limiting functions. Final temporal clauses also appear to fill pre-determined post-verbal slots and may alternate with prepositional phrases in narrowing verb reference.

4.4 Causal clauses as distinct from temporal and conditional clauses

While a sentence-level description of English would consider initial placement as available for all adverbial clauses, clauses introduced by *because* occur only finally in the present conversational corpus (see Schiffrin 1985 for a similar finding). The fact that *because*-clauses do not occur initially in this corpus suggests that the use of that position varies with genre, and may be a distinguishing feature of more planned language use.

To offer a sense of how initial placement is used in another genre of talk, here is a span of talk from a type of language use that is more unilaterally controlled and more planned than casual conversation. The excerpt is from an interview with feminist Charlotte Bunch, and it contains an initial *because*-clause used in a strategy reminiscent of the shift work of initial temporal and conditional clauses in the present conversational corpus. Bunch is discussing the Women's Party of the Philippines.

(20)
>They ran women candidates not just to win office but to bring another point of view.
>
>From what I know of them and the women who ran for office in Peru, it seems that women running for office in the Third World are much more clearly trying to influence both the other parties and the political process by doing that.
>
>I would like to see groups in the United States like the National Women's Political Caucus have a stronger emphasis on working out what sort of platforms women should run on. *Because the United States is so individualistic*, when women run for office you rarely see a feminist group or even a local Democratic club say, we support her because she stands for these feminist issues. It becomes so quickly an individualistic thing, do you like or do you don't like this woman.   (Douglas 1987)

In the discourse that precedes the initial *because*-clause, Bunch has described the women's movement in the Third World as emphasizing the development of a feminist platform, and she has expressed the desire to see US feminists adopt this approach. By introducing a contrast, the initial *because*-clause creates a connection with the point Bunch has made in her discussion of Third World feminist politics. The characterization of the US as *so individualistic* presents a contrast to the attitude in the Third World where Bunch sees points of view valued more highly than individual candidates. We can see, then, that in a non-conversational genre of talk, discourse can be organized and developed through the use of initial *because*-clauses. The absence of such usage in the present conversational data has to do with the type of work being done in the talk, and the lesser degree of planning that goes into it. While Bunch was probably prepared to talk about specific types of

Final adverbial clauses in continuous intonation

information in the interview, the speakers in the conversational corpus were not involved in presenting and developing particular points of view and arguments based on routine questions that arise from their areas of expertise, nor were they given as much time as they might need to develop any particular point. These differences lead to different features of language use, and, in this case, in initial placement of *because*-clauses in the interview, a more monologue genre, and the lack of initial placement of *because*-clauses in the conversational corpus.

As an alternative to introducing a cause with *because*, a cause can be placed before its consequence and linked to the consequence by *so*. Connecting causes and effects through a non-anticipatory linkage allows both causes and effects to span several clauses. In the following example, M is telling the story of what led to a fight at the races. What is at least in part a causal connection is made through *so* at the arrow.

(21)
    M: De Wa::ld spun ou:t. 'N he waited.
       (0.5)
    M: Al come around'n passed im, Al was leadin' the feature,
       (0.5)
    M: en' then the second- place guy,
       (0.8)
    M: an' then Keegan. An' boy when Keegan come around, he come right up into him, tried to put him into the wa:ll.
    C: Yeh?
    M: 'n he tried it about four different times, finally Keegan rapped him a good one in the a:ss'n the- b-De Wald went o:ff.
       (0.2)
    C: ⌈Mm
    M: ⌊But in the meantime it'd cost Keegan three spo:ts in the feature.
    C: Yeah?
→   M: So, boy when Keegan come in, he- yihknow how, he 's got a temper anyway, he js::: wa:::::h sc⌈reamed 'is =
    C: ⌊Mm
    M: =damn e:ngine yihknow,
       (0.5)
    M: settin' there an'he takes his helmet off'n, clunk it goes on top of the car, he gets out'n goes up t'the trailer 'n gets a god damn iron ba:r? .hhh r:aps that trailer an' away he starts t'go,

```
             an' everybody seh hey you don't need that y'know, seh ye:h
             you're right'n throws ⎡ that son'vabitch down- .hhhhhhh
     C:                            ⎣ Mm hm hm
                                                              (AD 10.23)
```

Notice that the *so* connects not just the immediately preceding and following clauses, but rather many clauses both before and after (see Schiffrin 1987 for a discussion of the discourse work of *so*). The aggravating actions by DeWald are described over a series of clauses, as are the actions that Keegan takes in response. If *because* were to introduce all the potentially causal material in this span of talk, it would require the listener to keep all that information in mind while waiting for the result.

In the cases of initial temporal and conditional clauses, on the other hand, the information presented as conditional or temporal limitation on the main clauses is, in most cases, easy to fit into a single clause, as in the following examples:

(22)
→   then, (0.7) .hhh um (0.4) w-when they were eating, (0.4) she mentioned something, about his spaghetti, being stuck together, an' so we started picking on him and his food,   (PJ 4.15)

(23)
     A: ... If you wanna leave about eleven, I'll walk down with you
        °'cause I have to go to school.   (TG 634)

When *because* appears between the result or the explainable assertion and the cause or explanation, what follows the *because* may also be multi-clausal. In example 24, M is commenting on the story he has been telling about the fight at the races. The *because* introduces a multi-clausal elaboration of the preceding assertion. The assertion that DeWald makes his first mistake by messing with a Keegan is followed by a causal link and some explanatory information.

(24)
→   M: But yihknow eh- un-he made his first mistake number one by messin' with Keegan, because a'pits'r fulla Keegans, an' when there isn't a Keegan, there there's a'Franks.   (AD 12.3)

In a measurement of temporal, conditional, and causal clause length, I found that temporal and conditional clauses were shorter than causals. As displayed in Table 9, conditional and temporal

Table 9. *Average word length of clauses*[5]

Temporal	Conditional	Causal
4	4	9

clauses average about four words in length (not counting the conjunction), while causal clauses average nine words.[6] Given the shorter average length of conditional and temporal clauses, the anticipatory use of such clauses is not likely to be as cognitively demanding as the anticipatory use of the longer causal clauses.

In addition to the option of using *so*, and the lengthy spans of talk that may be causally connected, there is one other feature of connected discourse that contributes to the avoidance of initial *because*-clauses in conversation. That is the possibility of inferring cause from sequence. Example 25 contains a case in point. At lines 3 and 4 the protagonist starts to go off with an iron bar, but then everyone says that he doesn't need the bar. At line 5, the protagonist responds with *Yeah you're right*, and throws down the bar.

(25)
```
1  M:  ...an'he takes his helmet off'n, clunk it
2      goes on top a' the car, he gets out'n goes up t'the
3      trailer 'n gets a god damn iron ba:r? .hhh r:aps that
4      trailer an' away he starts t'go, an' everybody seh hey
5      you don't need that y'know, seh ye:h you're right'n
6      throws [that son'vabitch down- .hhhhhhh       (AD 11.1)
```

The segment could have been presented using *because*:

(26)
→ ...but because everybody says, "Hey you don't need that," he says, "Yeah you're right" and he throws that son of a bitch down.
(hypothetical example)

or *so*:

(27)
→ and everybody says, "Hey you don't need that," so he says, "Yeah you're right" and he throws that son of a bitch down.
(hypothetical example)

However, the causal connection need not be explicity stated since it is inferable from the sequence of events.

In these data, then, *because* seems to function only as a link *between* causally related assertions, and does not function as an anticipatory link, introducing causal material to be followed by the associated result. I have suggested three factors which probably contribute to the lack of *because* used as an anticipatory link. First, English provides the easy option of using *so* as a connector for the pattern "cause plus result," an option which is used in these conversations to the exclusion of anticipatory *because*. Second, causal linkages appear between long units of talk, spans which might be cognitively taxing to process, both in production and comprehension, were the connection to be made in an anticipatory manner, with *because* preceding the entire causal section of talk. Third, causal connections between assertions are inferable from sequence. While conditional and temporal information may also be signaled by other means than adverbial conjunctions, there are no non-anticipatory conjunctions that may be said to signal exclusively temporal or conditional linkages. The reduction of *because* to a simple connector, alternating with *so* and used only between connected clauses and never as an anticipatory linkage, seems to be well-suited to this unplanned genre of language use.

Not only are *because*-clauses different from temporal and conditional clauses in appearing only finally, they also pattern differently with respect to their intonationally signaled connection to the prior material. *Because*-clauses follow final falling intonation more frequently than do temporal and conditional clauses. Table 10 shows the frequency of temporal and conditional clauses following continuing and final intonation as compared with the frequency of *because*-clauses following the same two contours.

Looking across the two rows, we see that *because*-clauses appear after the ending intonation 53% of the time, while temporal and conditional clauses follow ending intonation only 27% of the time. After continuing intonation, a majority of adverbial clauses are temporal or conditional (56%), while of the clauses following ending intonation a majority are causal (71%). The work that adverbial clauses do when they follow ending intonation is covered in chapter 5; this skewed distribution is cited here because it is another area of difference between the use of

Table 10. *Intonation of final temporal and conditional clauses versus final causal clauses*

	Continuing intonation	Ending intonation	Totals
Temporal and conditional	44 (73%) (56%)	16 (27%) (29%)	60 (100%)
Causal	35 (47%) (44%)	40 (53%) (71%)	75 (100%)
Totals	79 (100%)	56 (100%)	135

($X^2 = 8.69$, 1 d.f., $p < .005$)

because-clauses as opposed to temporal (*when, while, before, after,* etc.) and conditional (*if*) clauses. In addition to appearing only finally, *because*-clauses also differ from the temporals and conditionals in the frequency with which they are intonationally connected to the previous material.

One further indication of the difference between *because*-clauses and temporals and conditionals is the frequency of pauses and disfluencies (cut-off words, restarts, fillers) either before or after the conjunction when adverbial clauses are placed finally. Even when *because*-clauses are intonationally connected with the previous material, they are more likely than temporal and conditional clauses to display pauses and disfluencies. Examples 28 and 29 contain disfluencies and pauses before and after *because* or *'cause*.

(28)
→ K: Y'know in Los Altos, the::y were tryin' t'sue the city becuz- (0.1) (thi-) some women were, becuz- a:ll the street lights, were an ugly colored yellow, an' at ni:ght, (0.4) they make women, look really ugly. (SN 667)

(29)
→ P: Oh yeah you've gotta tell Mike tha:t, Uh-'cause they
⎡ want that on fi:lm.
K: ⎣ Oh: no: here we go ag(hh)ain, (AD 1.2)

Table 11. *Pauses and disfluencies in final temporals and conditionals versus causals*

	Pauses or disfluencies	No pauses or disfluencies	Totals
Temporals and conditionals	3 (7%)	41 (93%)	44 (100%)
Causals	8 (23%)	27 (77%)	35 (100%)
Totals	11	68	79

($X^2 = 2.95$, 1 d.f., $p < .10$)

Table 11 shows the frequency of pauses and disfluencies associated with final temporal and conditional adverbial clauses as opposed to causal adverbial connections (only clauses connected across continuing intonation contours are included). Causal connections are associated with pauses and disfluencies in 23% (8) of the cases while conditionals and temporals only display such features 7% (3) of the time (conditionals = 2, temporals = 1). While these numbers are small, in combination with the intonation pattern discussed above, the percentage difference is suggestive and it forms part of a total picture in which causal clauses are not tied as smoothly to the preceding material as are temporal and conditional clauses.

These differences all point to the less planned nature of *because*-clauses. As suggested in the discussion of initial placement of adverbial clauses, the use of initial position in an information management strategy can reflect planning and unilateral control of the floor. To use an initial adverbial clause as a point of realignment in the development of ideas, one must have its content well formulated. Likewise, to connect an assertion with a final adverbial clause across continuing intonation reflects, at the very least, that the main clause assertion was conceived of as incomplete itself; continuing intonation signals that there is more to come in relation to the grammatical unit that is coming to an end, and that the present utterance is still in progress. Pauses and disfluencies, too, are signs that the exact content of a unit of talk has not been selected or is at least being displayed as problematic. There is, then, a body of observations suggesting that clausal connections introduced by *because* are less planned than temporal and conditional connections.

With regard to the usage of patterns of *because*-clauses as opposed to temporal and conditional clauses, it seems that material introduced by *because* is more a product of interaction between speaker and recipient (this will be further supported in chapter 5). Speakers seem to make adequate predictions about the degree of temporal and conditional elaboration or limitation that any given assertion will need for comprehension by the listener. This is evidenced by the likelihood of temporal and conditional clauses to appear with their associated main clauses in pre-planned intonational packages. It seems to be less obvious that such information as is introduced by *because* should be included, as reflected in the likelihood of disfluencies or ending intonation in association with such connections. That temporal or conditional limitation is appropriate for an utterance seems to be easily predicted by speakers, but that an utterance needs some form of causal elaboration seems to be negotiated through the interaction itself.

We have seen, then, that *because*-clauses pattern differently from other adverbial clauses in these data: they appear only finally, behaving more like coordinating than subordinating conjunctions, and they are most likely to follow final intonation. In describing the placement of temporal and conditional clauses, a case was made for final position as the default location for such clauses when they are not involved in discourse organization. While *because*-clauses never appear in discourse organizationally significant initial position, they do operate in final position to introduce new information in several different ways. In section 4.4.2, I will outline the types of connections that *because* creates between intonationally unified clauses. Chapter 5 covers cases in which adverbial clauses follow ending intonation, including *because*-clauses.

4.4.2 Three types of causal connections

Looking only at *because* as a connector between intonationally continuous clauses, we find three types of discourse patterns: cases in which the content of the clause prior to the causal link contains a version of already shared information functioning as background for the causal information; cases in which the clause prior to the link contains cataphora, or references that point ahead for specification or elaboration; and cases in which both the clause prior to the causal link and the causal clause present entirely new information.

The first type of *because*-clause appears after a main clause that presupposes some information from the prior discourse. As was illustrated in the discussion of final temporal and conditional clauses, main clauses may serve the same pivotal, discourse-connecting functions as initial adverbial clauses. In such cases, the main clause creates the connection between prior talk and talk that follows. This type of discourse-connection pattern is also present among the occurrences of *because*-clauses in these data. In the following example, it has been suggested that C tell a particular joke that some of the friends have not yet heard. P agrees and encourages C to tell the joke. The main clause restates the suggestion, and the *because*-clause gives the reason or motivation, the new information in this context.

(30)
```
        P: Oh yeah you've gotta tell Mike tha:t, Uh-'cause they want that
           on fi:lm.                                          (AD 1.2)
```

In the talk that follows example 30, G says he doesn't want to hear the joke and K teases him about why he doesn't like the joke.

(31)
```
        G: I ⎡don't thin⎡k it's that funny.
        K:   ⎣Oh::,     ⎢
        P:              ⎣I gotta go t'the joh⎡n before I hear that again.
        K:                                   ⎣You'll like it,
           you'⎡ll really like it.
        C:     ⎣You do too y⎡ou laugh like hell you hhuh!
        P: ehheh huh
        G: Well I⎡:,
        C:       ⎣Y-
        G: had'n had a ⎡beer ye:t.
    →   K:             ⎣You don't like it, because you didn't
           think of it!                                       (AD 1.6–15)
```

Final adverbial clauses in continuous intonation 95

In the main clause of K's turn at the arrow, she restates that G doesn't like the joke, and the *because*-clause presents the new information, the reason why G doesn't like the joke.

In addition to restating prior information, another way a main clause can contain information that has already been given in the prior talk can be seen when a main clause presents a contrast or variation on some proposition in the prior talk. In the next example, N has suggested that she will buy her friend H a drink that evening. H agrees but qualifies how much she can drink:

(32)
```
      H: Maybe we can go out for a drink tonight.
          (.)
      N: Ye::ah. That soun-Yeh I owe y'a dri:nk.
          (.)
      N: Ah wanna buy y'a dri:n[k.
      H:                       [Aow. A'ri[:ght,
      N:                                 [Oka:y? So we will
          for sure. =
      H: =Ari[ght.
      N:    [After, (.) the pl[ay
      H:                      [.hh
          (.)
 →    H: I can't drink too much, 'cause I'm
          dri-i-vh[i(h)i(h)ng,
      N:         [Oka:y                        (HG 38.23)
```

H's main clause (at the arrow) presents the limitation on how much she can drink. This main clause takes the content of the prior discourse and presents a contrast. The *because*-clause adds the reason for the main clause shift, the new information.

In the next example H guesses at what drug N's doctor is giving her, *Tetracyclene?* N's answer, *No*, constitutes the "main clause" to which a following *because* is linked. N then gives an account for her negative response.

(33)
```
      N: So he gave me these pills to ta:ke?=
      H: =What. Tetracyclene?
          (.)
 →    N: PT No: 'cause I used to take that. An' it didn't he:lp. So he
          gave me something e:lse.=
      H: =Hm:.                                  (HG 4.16–20)
```

The *No* assumes the content of H's question, adding only negation. The explanation that is introduced by *'cause* is the new information.

In cases of presupposed main clauses, the continuing intonation signals the speaker's recognition that the main clause does not constitute the complete message the utterance is meant to convey; the main clause links the new information in the adverbial clause back to the prior talk.

In another set of cases of final causals, while the main clause assertion is not presupposed, it could not stand alone in its context, but points beyond itself for completion. These main clauses function as a pre-evaluation of the material that will follow *because*:

(34)
```
     C:   I knew he was gonna go, on this thing. N' (0.2) an' I- (.) an' he
          was rea:lly sick. But I didn't want to be like (.) the momma, an'
          say don't go. Go ahead. You'll have a good time, it's all right.
          Next da:y, he was esco:rted home, by (hh) ⎡ (he was) =
     W:                                             ⎣ On a stretcher?
     C:   Just abou:t.
              (1.2)
     W:   How awful. ⎡ Oh: Go:d.
     H:              ⎣ Uhh.
              (1.0)
→    C:   It's interesting, y'know 'cause th- the (0.8) frie:nds(.) we had,
          would always act like oh, how could you get si:ck, y'know
          you guys are wimpy westerners. But (.) Gee:ven, ( ) the guy
          who bought them ba:ck, knew exa:ctly (.) he an' I went out
          immediately, while David sort of sprawled on the bed, (0.7)
          immediately, an' got three different things that they: al:ways
          use:, when they're sick. Which is, quite often, I think.
          (Y'know) he went to the pharmacy, he knew just what to ask
          for:, they get sick too:                              (AM 188)
```

In this example, *it's interesting* is cataphoric. Though *it's* could be pointing back to the prior discussion of D's illness in Nepal, what is *interesting* is yet to be explained. The continuing intonation reflects C's plan to elaborate on what was interesting, and *'cause* introduces a lengthy elaboration in the form of a story. In fact, this particular usage of *'cause* is functioning less as a causal conjunction and more as a part of an idiom in which the slot filled here by *'cause* might instead be filled by *that*[7]:

It's interesting $\begin{bmatrix}\text{'cause}\\\text{that}\end{bmatrix}$ the friends we had would...

A main clause can also point beyond itself by presenting a strong assertion that the speaker believes will not be self-evident in its context or to the particular listeners involved. In the next example, M, the man most experienced with the local car racing scene, has been talking about a fight that happened at the track the night before. He now makes a comment on the story and explains the comment in a series of clauses initially introduced by *because*.

(35)
```
     1  M:  But yihknow eh- un-he made his first mistake number
→    2      one by messin' with Keegan, because a'pits'r fulla
     3      Keegans, an' when there is ⌈n't a Keegan, there,
     4      there's a' 'Fra ⌈:nks.       ⌊
     5  C:          ⌊                    Mmhm,
     6  C:          ⌊ There's a'Fra:nks,
     7  M:  ⌈( )=
     8  C:  ⌊(I kno:⌈w.)
     9  M:          ⌊=Because they're related, yihkno:w?
                                                        (AD 12.4)
```

The assertion about the antagonist's *first mistake* is stated strongly; it has heightened emphasis created through a combination of pre- and post-modification, *first* comes before *mistake* and *number one* follows it. The strongly stated assertion serves to introduce the explanation that follows the *because*.

This example is especially interesting in that it shows how, for the interlocutors, the prediction of what is and is not shared information cannot be easily judged where causal elaborations are concerned. Explaining something that a listener already knows is interactionally significant and can be taken as condescension. Notice that the explanation of why this was the *first mistake* is not entirely new to C. In his second utterance, at line 6, C collaboratively completes M's final clause, thus displaying his prior access to that information. Note also that C says something that the transcriber hears as *I know*, at line 8. Both these turns by C suggest that M was not entirely correct in his judgment that his assertion about the *first mistake* needed explanation. Judgment as to whether an assertion needs causal support is not straightforward, and the addition of causal elaboration often arises through interaction (as will be further discussed in chapter 5).

In the majority of the cases of causal clauses after continuing intonation, the content of the two clauses is asserted jointly, with neither clause presupposed or pointing beyond itself. In one such example, P reports on another incident involving the car driver who started the fight the night before. P's report comes as part of the commentary after the fight story, and represents more support for seeing DeWald, the villain in the story, as a bad fellow.

(36) (Simplified)
    P: Mike said he used to: race gocarts, en' he got <u>barred</u> from the gocart track, because he ra:n little kids off the <u>track</u>.
                                                                 (AD 13.11)

Here, the fact that the driver was barred from the track could be news in itself, but presented with the cause, the assertion becomes a clearer piece of evidence of the fact that the man is mean.

Example 37, below, also contains two pieces of new information that are presented as a unit. The news is not just that the man was almost arrested, but that he was almost arrested for a specific reason.

(37)
    M: I went out one night with my friend Do:n?
       (0.2)
    S: Yeah.
    M̶: A:nd uh: (0.4) He was almost arrested at a ba:r, because he didn't have his eye dee:?
       (0.2)
    M: There's a-friend of ours had it 'n his po:cket? .hhh Then after that he gets in a car and was so furious that he smashed in to the back of another car.   (SN 393)

A jointly asserted causal complex involves the judgment that a main clause only makes sense in combination with the content of the causal clause. As can be seen in the next example, such a judgment can be in error. H is talking about how she found out about a play she and N are going to see that night.

(38)
    H: I was looking in the Calendar section an' there was u:n, (.) an a:d yihknow a little: u-thi:ng, .hh⌈hh
    N: ⌊<u>Uh</u>hu:h=

```
    H: At- th'-the theater's called the Met Theater, it's
       on Point⎡ setta
    N:        ⎣ The Me:t,
       (.)
    N: I never heard of i⎡ t.
    H:                    ⎣ I hadn't either. .hhh But
       anyways, u-en theh the moo- thing was the Dark at
       the Top a the Stai⎡ :rs.
    N:                   ⎣ Mm-h m⎡ :
    H:                            ⎣ An' I nearly went c(h)razy,
→   'cause I:⎡ l::o:ve that mo:vie.
    N:        ⎣ y:Yeah I know you lo:ve tha::t.    (HG 8.10)
```

H delivers the main and causal clauses together as a joint assertion, supposing that both clauses present new information, but as it turns out N recognizes the motivation for H's *nearly going crazy*. As H delivers the causal clause, N overlaps with a display of recognition encoding the same content as H's clause.

4.4.3 Summary of final causal clauses

In section 4.4, I have presented a case for the difference between *because*-clauses and temporal or conditional clauses by reference to the differing patterns of placement, intonation, and disfluencies in delivery.

I have also categorized causal connections into three types. Causal elaborations may follow clauses that present some partially or fully presupposed information. They may elaborate and specify the meaning of either cataphoric reference or a strongly stated assertion in a preceding clause. And causal clause complexes may present unified causal assertions, involving neither presupposed

Table 12. *Final causal clauses after continuing intonation*

Following shared information	Elaborating cataphora or strong assertions	Two clauses of new information	Total
10 (29%)	4 (11%)	21 (60%)	35 (100%)

information nor cataphoric reference, but rather two clauses of new information.

4.5 Summary

This chapter has covered the occurrences of final adverbial clauses that appear between intonationally coherent units of talk, comparing the use of these final adverbial clauses to the use of initial adverbial clauses. We have seen that final adverbial clauses following continuing intonation are of a different discourse status than initial adverbial clauses. When, as is commonly the case, discourse is organized through connections between main clauses, adverbial clauses serve only to limit and qualify main clause reference in post-verbal positions. The results of analysis were given here in the form of exemplification based on a case-by-case examination of all the occurrences of final adverbial clauses after non-final intonation.

Quantified evidence was also offered in support of the observation that initial placement of adverbial clauses tends to be used in spans of talk controlled by single speakers. Final position, as the default location for adverbial clauses, does not require that any special rights to the floor be gained before its function becomes felicitous.

Temporal and conditional clauses were treated here separately from causal clauses, due to the fact that only the former two clause types were placed initially in this conversational corpus. *Because* was not used as an anticipatory conjunction, but instead alternated with *so* in expressing causal connections.

Clauses connected by *because* across continuing intonation contours were found to be different not only in their distribution, but also with respect to their intonation and the frequency with which they display disfluencies. Interactional sequences were cited in support of the observation that, as compared with the inclusion of temporal or conditional qualification, the inclusion of causal elaboration is more problematic and more likely to result from speaker recipient negotiation.

In this chapter, we have seen that in final position after continuing intonation, adverbial clauses generally provide new information and complete the information from their associated main clauses. The next chapter deals with final adverbial clauses produced after a preceding utterance has been completed with final intonation. These adverbial clause connections regularly arise in the contexts of self-editing and the negotiation of understanding between conversationalists.

5

Final adverbial clauses after ending intonation

5.1 Overview

In the previous two chapters I described the use of adverbial clauses presented in intonationally coherent packages with their associated main clauses. In the present chapter I examine cases involving grammatical connection through adverbial conjunctions, but in which the conjunction introduces a separate intonation unit. These adverbial clauses follow utterances ending in some form of final intonation, either low-falling or high-rising.

As described in chapter 4, final adverbial clauses following continuing intonation serve information-completing functions, narrowing clause meaning. Final adverbial clauses that follow ending intonation, though displayed through conjunctions to be extensions of previous units, also represent separate units in their own right. As will be seen in this chapter, these added-on adverbial clauses have clear interactional origins.

Adverbial clauses that are added after ending intonation have been referred to as "afterthoughts" (Chafe 1984). This term suggests that a unit of talk was originally planned not to include the adverbial clause, but that, after the unit was completed, the speaker decided to add another element of modification or elaboration. In the present chapter, I argue that, in addition to representing the editing of a speaker's talk based on her/his own thought process, such final adverbial clauses may also be the products of speaker–recipient negotiation specifically aimed at achieving interactional ends. There are specific conversational contexts in which speakers present a main clause plus adverbial elaboration in separated intonation units. The manner in which a speaker becomes

Table 13. *Final adverbial clauses added to possibly complete utterances*

	Temporal	Conditional	Causal	Concessive	Total
Same speaker	5	4	34	2	45
Different speaker	2	2	6		10
Total	7	6	40	2	55

aware that more might be added to an already completed unit often involves feedback from the other participants in the conversation. Adverbial clauses following ending intonation often come at the possible locations for speaker change or after recipients have provided some sign of disbelief, lack of understanding or other trouble. Final adverbial clauses after ending intonation are frequently parts of sequences in which a speaker is attempting to get a response from a recipient, and is having problems in doing so. Furthermore, there are contexts in which speakers present adverbial elaboration under separate intonation contours *not* as afterthoughts resulting from faulty planning, but as *deliberately* separate acts, with associated interactional significance.

This chapter, then, examines the circumstances in which a unit that has just been displayed as both grammatically and intonationally complete is re-opened grammatically by an adverbial conjunction. I will call such adverbial clauses *post-completion extensions* (hereafter PCEs).

As will become evident from the examples cited, *because* is the most frequent conjunction used to introduce added on material. This is related to the overall pattern of *because* connections in this corpus. *Because* introduces background, motivating, or explanatory material. Judging from the present corpus, such material is most likely to warrant separate intonational presentation, presentation as a separate unit of information (also see Chafe 1987).

Section 5.2 covers the occurrences of PCEs produced by the same speakers who produced the utterances that are qualified or elaborated upon. These constitute the majority of final adverbials following ending intonation (n = 45). Section 5.3 reviews the interactional contexts in which recipients, rather than same speakers, employ adverbial clauses in their responses, and in that way connect their responses to the previous speaker's talk (n = 10).

5.2 Adverbial clause extensions by same speakers

While the adverbial clauses described in the previous chapters involved modification within a single, intonationally connected utterance, adverbial clauses that follow final intonation are, in interactional terms, new units of talk. In conversation, after an utterance has been displayed as both grammatically and intonationally complete, another speaker may take the cue and begin her or his next turn, even if that turn merely displays the receipt of information, as in example 1 below.

(1)
    C: She decided to go a<u>wa</u>y this weekend.
    I: Yea:h, (TS 1.23)

When an utterance has been displayed as possibly complete, this is a signal to the recipient that the discourse up to the point of completion may now be processed as a finished unit. The completion of such a discourse unit may also be the completion of an interactional unit, a turn. Such completions, then, involve an orientation toward speaker change. The conversational turn-taking system, as described by Sacks *et al.* (1974), operates on what these researchers have called "turn-constructional units": "sentential, clausal, phrasal and lexical constructions" (1974:12). Units added on to previously completed utterances need not be full clauses. However, the turn-constructional units at issue in the present study are what in traditional grammatical terms are referred to as dependent and independent clauses (but see Longacre and Thompson 1985, Matthiessen and Thompson 1988).

After the first grammatical and intonational unit of talk in a speaker's turn has been completed, speaker change regularly occurs, unless the same speaker adds more to his or her own talk. Cases of same speaker continuation must, however, be arrived at cooperatively; other speakers must refrain from coming in at the point of discourse completion in order for the original speaker to add the next unit of talk.[1]

Each point of grammatical and intonational completion in a conversationalist's talk, then, is a point for the negotiation of who will speak next. These points, in fact, are points at which recipients provide signals of receipt (*MmHm*, *Yeah*, etc.) and at which overlapping talk frequently occurs. They are also points at which the original speaker may smoothly and without hesitation add units to her or his talk. The fact that the same speakers regularly do continue their turns suggests that the parties to conversation can project beyond grammatically and intonationally bounded units and perceive when longer units of talk are in progress. Such is the case with interactionally achieved primary speakership as discussed in chapter 4 (section 4.3.3). Points at which grammar and intonation signal unit completion are consequential for both discourse processing and interactional turn-taking.

The possibility of negotiated turn extension is relevant to an understanding of cases in which an adverbial clause is added after an utterance, and possibly a turn, has been treated as complete intonationally. While speakers cannot alter the intonation they have already produced, they do have the option of starting the next unit of talk with a connector that marks the new unit as a continuation of the utterance that has just been marked as complete. For instance, in example 2, N's turn contains three clauses. The second clause is connected to the first across a continuing intonation boundary; the third comes after the previous utterance has been intonationally marked as complete. Note that the second clause is not introduced with a connector, while the third clause is.

(2)
    H: Yeah but what you ea:t, if you eat greasy foo:d,
→   N: We:h he said it's no:t the fact that you've eaten the greasy food, it's the fact that you worry about it. And that makes you break ou:t.   (HG 5.7–10)

The connector introducing the third clause, *and*, explicitly marks that clause as a continuation of the prior utterance, even though that utterance has already been marked as complete intonationally. In the next example, a new clause is added to one already intonationally marked as complete, but this time the new clause is not introduced by a connector.

(3)
>C: Al's a pretty damn good driver. He's been around for a little while, (AD 19.14)

It is beyond the scope of the present research to analyze the circumstances in which a connector is or is not used (but see Schiffrin 1987); these examples are cited to give a picture of the options a speaker has for adding a unit of talk after the previous unit has been displayed as possibly complete, both grammatically and intonationally. When an adverbial clause follows a possibly completed utterance, the new unit of talk is displayed to be a continuation of the prior utterance. The speaker is showing that s/he sees the prior utterance as meriting some further qualification or elaboration before it can be considered properly finished.

There are various conversational contexts in which previously completed utterances are extended by adverbial clauses. Post-completion extensions are most often related to the *preference structure* at work in a particular interactional sequence. Preference structure (introduced in 1.1.3) is a system observed to operate in conversation whereby participants strive to maintain agreement in talk. Turns are built to be hearable as oriented toward certain response types. One can observe, for example, that a question may be built to be answered by *yes* rather than *no* (e.g., "You are coming to dinner, aren't you?"). When speakers build turns that prefer given types of responses on the parts of recipients, but such responses do not seem to be forthcoming, speakers regularly change their turns, by addition, to increase the likelihood that agreement will be reached. In the example below (from Sacks 1987), agreement with A's first question would be in the form of a *yes*, but when a pause, rather than a response, follows, A makes a new question, this time adapted to a *no* agreement.

(4)
>A: They have a good cook there?
> ((pause))
>A: Nothing special?
>B: No, everybody takes their turns. (Sacks 1987:64)

Thus, speakers signal the types of responses they expect, and they may adapt their talk when such a response is not forthcoming. The adaptation of a first pair part (a turn regularly followed by a second part by the recipient) is aimed at achieving agreement, making it easier for the recipient to agree.

Another aspect of preference structure is that, when a participant does not provide an agreeing response, there is a distinct shape to the disagreeing or dispreferred response. Among the features of dispreferred responses are delays, prefaces and accounts (Levinson 1983). That is, preferred responses tend to come quickly after the previous speaker ends her/his turn (without delay); they tend to be direct (without preface); and they do not necessitate explanation (without account). In the following example, we see B delivering a dispreferred response beginning with a delay, followed by *Well* (which can in fact function as a marker of a dispreferred response), then a preface of appreciation and the dispreferred response itself, *I don't think I can make it* . . . Note the account that follows, where B gives the reason for the refusal.

(5)
    A: Uh if you'd care to come and visit a little while this morning I'll give you a cup of coffee
    B: hehh Well that's awfully sweet of you, I don't think I can make it this morning. .hh uhm I'm running an ad in the paper and- and uh I have to stay near the phone.
(Atkinson and Drew 1979)

Preference structure plays a clear role in the interactional contexts of PCEs, both in terms of the shaping of first turns (first pair parts) and in the shaping of responses (second pair parts).

In section 5.2.1, I show the ways in which adverbial clauses as PCEs arise from interaction. They form extensions of prior turns when some sign of trouble is evident or when a recipient has provided a prompt for further explanation. They also form the account portions of dispreferred turns.

In section 5.2.2, I review the cases of adverbial clauses added on at the possible locations for speaker change, but which are added without such obvious displays of trouble from recipients.

5.2.1 *Prompted final adverbial clauses*

In example 6 below, containing a prompted adverbial clause PCE, we see a question added onto with a causal elaboration. A question is a prototypical first pair part, calling for a response by another speaker. The short beat of silence that comes after the question represents an interactionally significant delay in uptake (Pomerantz 1978, 1984). As a result, A adds an adverbial clause PCE which provides background for his question. R has been telling A about some chest pain he has been having.

(6)
    A: .hhh <u>W</u>ell do ya think it's: umm (0.2) ahm (0.2) <u>stress</u>?
        (.)
→   'Cause a lot a <u>back</u>- I know <u>back pain</u>, (0.2) <u>comes</u> with stress.
    R: .hhh <u>We</u>:ll I'm <u>thinking</u> it <u>might</u> be uhh (0.2) I um: (0.5)
       I <u>haven't</u> ever <u>had</u>- ahh directly related <u>physical symptoms</u> of
       <u>stress before</u>, and it could <u>easily</u> be <u>that</u>,   (YG 99)

Note that R's response is hesitant, and it is certainly not a clear agreement, beginning with the pre-dispreferred marker, *well*. Thus, A's decision to add an explanation to his question is well-motivated; his recipient is not able to provide a thoroughly agreeing response even after the PCE.

In the next example, S is beginning to tell a story about a friend who collected insurance money from the owners of the building where the people in this conversation live. S is trying to establish shared understanding of what the problematic dripping is. She expects that the others will recognize what she is talking about and prompts their recognition with upward intonation. It is not, however, until she adds on a second try, introduced by *if*, that she gets the response, *mm hm*.

(7) (La Mancha is the name of the apartment building the students live in)
    S: La Mancha had something <u>dri</u>:pping on the front of <u>my</u> car last year, but I never got to collect on it.
       (0.2)
    S: Yihknow when it- (.) came from the:: I think (a) air conditioning system, it drips on the front of the ca:rs?
       (.)
→ S: If you park in a certain place?
    (R): Mm hmm   (SN 460)

Again, a beat of silence precedes the PCE. This beat seems to be enough to encourage an extension in pursuit of a response displaying recognition.

Final adverbial clauses after ending intonation 109

It is not only after pauses (the absence of response) that we find PCEs. When a recipient responds, it may not be the response that the speaker is pursuing and may, thus, elicit a PCE. In the next example, first we find a pause leading to an added causal phrase and later a minimal receipt marker prompting another PCE.

(8)
```
    1        (4.0)
    2   K:   It was like the other day uh,
    3        (0.2)
    4        Vera (.) was talking on the phone to her mom?
    5   C:   Mm hm.
    6   K:   An uh she got off the pho:ne, an she was
    7        incredibly upset?
    8   C:  ⌈Mm hm.⌉
    9   K:  ⌊She wz goin⌋ God, do you think they're (.)
   10        performing unnecessary surgery on my dad, or
   11        some'm like that?
   12        (0.2)
→  13   K:   Just 'cause uh some'm her mom had told her.
   14        (0.5)
   15   K:   It was really amazing.= (It wz all) you know like
   16        Nazi experiments or something.(sd) God he wouldn't
   17        be in there, (0.2) if he didn't need it ya know?=
   18   C:   =Ye⌈a:h.
→  19   K:      ⌊If it wasn't some'm real. Ya know?
   20        (0.2)
   21   C:   W-have you met his doctor?
   22   K:   (Js the woman call⌈ing her)
   21   V:                      ⌊I met no-not- I met the
   22        doctor that assisted.                              (K 1)
```

We can see that from lines 1–11 K is making a report and ending each increment of that report with upward, question intonation, making a special appeal for receipt markers from C, the only other person to whom K's report is news (the story concerns V, the other party to the conversation). C provides appropriate receipt markers at lines 5 and 8, but at line 12 there is no response. The pause is taken by K as a signal of trouble, and it prompts an added causal phrase, which comes at line 13, introduced by *just 'cause*. The causal phrase that is added on here makes explicit the relationship that is implicit in the sequence of events reported. V talked on the phone to her mom, and when she got off she was very upset: the phone call caused the upset. Due to the lack of response at line 12, K states the implicit cause with the modification of *just*, emphasizing that although this was the cause, it hardly merits the type of emotional reaction V gave it. While this added unit is not an adverbial clause, and is, therefore, not counted as a causal PCE in this study, it is interesting to note that the interactional context of the emergence of this phrasal addition is quite similar to the contexts of adverbial clause PCEs discussed in this section.[2]

Even after K has made explicit that it was the call which made V so upset and that he does not think her reaction was appropriate, C still withholds her response; at line 14 we see another pause. This pause is followed by K's very clear evaluation of the report at line 15, *It was really amazing*. If C has not yet understood that K is asking her to express her amazement at V's behavior, she should understand after this evaluation. And in fact C does, at last, give a token of receipt at line 18. However, K overlaps this token with an adverbial clause PCE.

While the PCEs in examples 6 and 7 were prompted by pauses or lack of response, the conditional PCE in example 8 comes after C has begun to provide a receipt marker. In the context of K's full report, C's minimal receipt marker at line 18 is not only late but inadequate. K is pursuing a stronger response, one more sympathetic to the tone of his report. K's talk involves a complaint: V is characterized as overreacting to her mother's call. This is displayed in the strong terms K uses to describe the sequence of events: *She was incredibly upset* and *It was really amazing... like Nazi experiments*. After such a strongly stated negative report, C's minimal receipt token, *Yea:h*, prompts K to add another increment to his turn, still hoping to get the right reaction from C. Such a response does not come, however, and after yet another pause, C gives V a chance to defend herself, asking about V's knowledge of the medical situation in question (line 21).

Example 8, then, shows how it is not only a pause, or missing response, that can prompt an adverbial clause PCE. We see that an overt but minimal response, if it is not the one being pursued in the talk (i.e., the preferred response), can create a context in which a speaker extends her/his turn with a PCE.

Final adverbial clauses after ending intonation 111

Let me offer another example in which a pause alone prompts an adverbial PCE. In this instance, the pause is after an increment of information has been given; the speaker waits for a signal of receipt. With none forthcoming after a short pause, a causal PCE is added. What is particularly interesting here is that the trouble that A picks up from the pause alone is confirmed by the question that the recipient asks, overlapping with the PCE. A is telling R about his situation working at a television studio.

(9)

```
       A: .hhh but the thing is, the- they might get thei:r (0.2) the
          project ca:ncelled.
  →         (0.2)
  →    A: becau:se ⎡(they)
  →    R:          ⎣What this (.) wa:r project?=
       A: =Yeah because hhh ABC got bought ou:t?
            (0.6)
       A: Didcha hear about tha:t?=
       R: =Ye:ah,
       A: .hhh An' that they're real tight wa:ds?         (AR 263)
```

The pause comes at a possible place for a receipt token from R. The lack of such a token may be a signal that the information has not been adequately heard or understood by the recipient. At the second arrow, we see A beginning a PCE, to extend the utterance he has previously marked as complete. Overlapping with A's PCE, R delivers a question, specifically a *next turn repair initiator* (NTRI). NTRIs are recipient prompts that signal lack of understanding or hearing. They appear in the recipient turn following a trouble spot (Schegloff, Jefferson and Sacks 1977). The fact that R overlaps A's incipient explanation with a repair initiator (at the third arrow) confirms that the pause was indeed a sign of trouble. The trouble R targets involves the reference of *the project*: whereas A had treated it as a definite referent, assumed to be shared by the recipient, R is not sure of the referent. With the *Yeah* that follows R's question, A confirms R's guess as to the reference. A then goes on to an extension of the original news by means of *because* plus a piece of background information. This PCE is delivered with rising intonation, in an attempt to prompt some signal that R shares the background necessary to understand why the project may be canceled. In fact A's last two turns in this excerpt continue to invite a response from R that will validate that shared background has been established.

In example 9, then, we find one aborted PCE introduced by *because*, and one complete PCE also introduced by *because*. The first *because* is responsive to the pause after the delivery of a piece of information, and the second is part of an effort to establish a shared background of information for the news. The second *because* may simply be a completion of what A started with the first. He may have made a guess at the problem represented by the pause, and decided that more overall background was necessary. Then, even after R has designated a more limited kind of trouble (one item of reference), A continues to add background. As we will see below (section 5.2.2), within a single turn, without a pause, a speaker may use *because* to introduce background to utterances previously treated as complete. Thus, adverbial PCEs may be prompted both by pauses and by repair initiators, repair initiators being outright targeting of trouble, while pauses are more subtle displays that elaboration may be needed.

Example 10, below, is another case in which a repair initiator prompts an adverbial PCE. N asks a question that H does not hear or understand properly. At the first arrow, the two parenthetical transcriptions represent possible hearings of something difficult to parse. The turn that the transcriber has trouble with is the same turn which leads to the NTRI.

```
(10)
          H: Getting my hair cut tomorrow,=
          N: =Oh really?
               (.)
          H: Yea: ⎡:::h,
    →     N:      ⎣Oh (fer foo:d?)
                   (so soo:d?)
    →          (0.4)
          H: Wha:t?
               (0.2)
    →     N: 'Cause 'member you said you w⎡ere g'nna make=
          H:                               ⎣whhhhhhhoo
          N: =an appo⎡intment,
          H:         ⎣O h: yaah. Yihknow what I thought
              you sai:d .hh=
          N:   =⎡Wha:t,
          H:    ⎣for foo:d, hhhhh⎡hhhhhhh              (HG 16.11)
```

The first sign that H is having trouble with N's question (at the second arrow) is the pause that follows the question. This pause is at the location where H's response is expected to be if she has heard and understood the question, and if she has no particular problem with answering it. The pause, then, indicates that some problem exists. H then provides a clear display of her trouble with the NTRI just after the pause, *What?*. The pause that follows that is a sign that N is having difficulty deciding what particular trouble H's NTRI points to; *What?* targets the whole prior utterance for repair, giving no hint as to whether any part of the utterance has been understood. At the last line of the example, we can see that H did in fact hear *for* plus some noun. Instead of *What?*, H could have provided an NTRI such as *For food?*. This would have given N more information as to what aspect of her talk had been misunderstood.

The adverbial clause that N provides at the third arrow is evidence of her interpretation of the problem. She assumes that H has understood the words, but not the reason behind her asking the question. Based on that interpretation, she introduces the background and motivation for her question through the conjunction *'cause*.[3] N was surprised that H had gotten an appointment *so soon*.

In example 10, as in 9, after trouble has been signaled through a pause, the recipient makes the problem explicit through a repair initiator. This leads to a turn by the original speaker which is introduced by *because*. Again, the conjunction can be heard as both responding to the NTRI, and extending the speaker's previous turn.

Finally, the most obvious way that a listener can prompt the addition of an adverbial clause to another speaker's talk is through a direct question. In example 11, H is catching N up on the current events in H's life. At this point, H is talking about a male friend from whom she has not heard in a while.

(11)
    H: There's something else I was gonna say ⎡Oh yeah.=
    N: ⎣Oh:.
    H: =.hhhahh
        (0.2)
    H: I yihknow when: e-nyeh I was deciding, if I should write him

```
                the thankyou no:te,  ⎡for the birthday
                gi:ft, hh .hh=       ⎢
        N:                           ⎣Y e a : h
→       H:  =I decided no:t to.  ⎡Thou-ough.
→       N:                       ⎣H o w  c o:me,=
        H:  = .t .hhhhhhh
            (.)
→       H:  Because I figure,hhhhhh  ⎡hhh
        N:                           ⎣If he  ⎡hasn't written ye:t,
        (H:)                                 ⎣(He-)
            (0.4)
        N:  then he doesn't want to.                    (HG 29.3)
```

In this sequence, H first reminds N of the context, the fact that H was deciding whether to write. She then provides the outcome, which, through the final *though*, she displays as being counter to what was expected (first arrow). H's turn is built to be taken as surprising, counter to expectation. The fact that the outcome was not expected is displayed in N's reaction: simultaneous with H's delivery of *though*, N asks the question, *How come* (second arrow). N did not need the conjunct *though* to display the news as counter to expectation and warranting further explanation.

In this example, as in the two preceding ones, *because* introduces an answer that can be taken as an extension of the speaker's previous utterance, as well as a direct answer to the question, *How come*. Again the conjunction has a dual function, relating back both to the other speaker's talk and to the same speaker's talk.

Examples 8 through 11 have involved the extension of turns when recipients do not respond in the preferred manner. There is another way in which preference structure is involved in the presentation of adverbial clauses as separate intonation units. As discussed above, in dispreferred responses, accounts often follow the non-agreeing part of the turn. Such accounts may be introduced by *because* or *'cause* and appear under new intonation contours.

There is a group of cases of causal adverbial PCEs, then, that come as extensions of dispreferred responses, responses that are analyzably not what the previous speaker's turn was meant to receive. Example 12 below is such a case. A asks R a question that prefers an affirmative response. This preference is underscored by the expression, *at least*, which is overlapped by R's response:

(12)
    A: Did you get ye:r (.) your first pay check from it?
       (.)
    A: ⌈at least?
    R: ⌊NO: I won't get that for a couple weeks yet.=
    A: Oh,
       (.)
    A: ⌈W'l
→   R: ⌊'Cause it takes a long time.
    A: At least it's in the bank,
       (0.5)
    R: Yeah it <u>will</u> be.   (AR 97)

This PCE resembles those already discussed, in that it follows some intervening talk by the recipient. The response is minimal, *Oh*, and the fact that the original question was built to prefer a *yes* remains to be addressed. R's causal PCE, then, supplies what is displayed to be an account for the dispreferred response. *It takes a long time* by itself could be taken as a negative assessment, but R is presenting it as an objective clarification or justification for the fact that he has not received a pay check yet — a fact that runs counter to her interlocutor's expectation. That the extension is introduced by *'cause* ensures that the account will not be taken as a complaint.

In the next example, V has been explaining (with some help from K) the knee operation that her father has just had and that her mother is upset about. C asks a question to clarify what part of the operation V's mother feels was unnecessary:

(13)
    K: It's like the bone ul- they cut the wedge out like this, 'n then pushed the bone down.
    C: Oh::=
    V: =So it's straight- it's- ⌈[it's- i]t's out like <u>that</u> now.
    C: ⌊That's a<u>ma</u>zing.]
    C: Is that what your mom thought was unnecessary
       ⌈°(now)?
→   V: ⌊No <u>she</u>: thinks that the whole thing's unnecessary.
→   'Cause h⌈e-he's in <u>so</u> much pain, that it seems=
            ⌊(Oh yeah)
    V: =like he's never gonna <u>walk</u> again. An' she's saying his leg's gonna be an inch shor:ter?
    K: °teh Oh shit.   (K 120)

With a general preference for agreement operating in conversation, V's negative response at the first arrow makes some form of account relevant. Such an account is introduced by *'cause*, after the correction that follows *No*. Again, a causal conjunction is used to introduce an account following a dispreferred response.

Example 14, below, is a final example of a causal conjunction introducing an account following a dispreferred response. A is trying to convince B to come into the city the following day. In this fragment (also discussed in chapter 3), A suggests a possible plan contingent on B's agreeing to come to town with A the next day. B has been consistently hesitant in her responses up to this point, and, at the arrow, we find the pre-dispreferred marker, *Well*, followed by another hesitation, *yihknow* and finally a negative response, *I don't want to make anything definite*.

(14)
```
        A:  Maybe if you come down, I'll take the car (then)
        B:  t! We:ll, uhd-yihknow I-I don' wanna make any- thing
    →       definite. Because I-yihknow I jus:: I jus::t thinkin:g today all
            day riding on th'trai:ns,
            hhuh-uh .hh ⌈h
        A:              ⌊Well there's nothing else to do.      (TG 685)
```

B's response is prototypically dispreferred, and an account is, once again, introduced by a causal conjunction (at the arrow).

What we have seen in this section is that adverbial clause PCEs can be understood by reference to the general system of preference structure observed to operate in conversations. PCEs may come as additions to turns when there is indication that the turn is not receiving the preferred response from the interlocutor. PCEs may also follow non-agreeing responses, introducing the predictable account that is a standard feature observed in dispreferred second turns.

In the next section, we will see how a speaker may add an adverbial clause after final intonation but in the absence of any sign of trouble, i.e., not following a pause, a recipient prompt, or a dispreferred response.

5.2.2 *Final adverbial clauses in the absence of obvious interactional trouble*

In the previous section we saw that adverbial clause PCEs could originate in obvious trouble with respect to the preference structure of conversational interaction. It is also possible that a speaker can perceive some trouble in the interaction before the trouble has become overt. This pattern has been observed in invitations, offers, requests, and proposals (Davidson 1984). In such cases, a speaker may end an utterance with final intonation, but then provide a PCE before a pause or recipient prompt has intervened.

One environment in which PCEs are provided before a prompt is evident involves first pair parts, or turns that clearly call for certain responses on the parts of recipients. These cases are similar to cases discussed in 5.2.1, but the PCEs here come without intervening pauses or recipient turns (at least no pause that was perceptible to the transcribers).

In example 15 below, M is responding to a strange story reported by K. At the arrow, M asks a question that displays his surprise. There is no hearable pause after this question, but M nevertheless adds a PCE to clarify the question:

(15)
```
    K:  Y'know in Los Altos, the::y were tryin' t'sue the city, becuz-
        (0.1) thi- some women were, becuz- (0.2) all the street lights,
        were an ugly colored yellow, en at ni:ght, (0.4) they make
        women, look really ugly.
        (1.0)
    K:  An' they wanted t'sue:.
    S:  'Cause it hur⌈ts business?
    K:          ⌊'Cause there was NO WO⌈MEN WOULD GO
        OU:T (at night)
    R:                  ⌊uh huh huh
    S:  Compensation for bad business.=
    K:  =Ye⌈ah(h)hh
    R:     ⌊mmh hmh,
        (0.2)
    K:  (I d'know what i-)
        (0.5)
```

→   M: Are you serious? ⌈Because there was (yellow) li:ght?
    K: ⌊I'm serious
        (0.3)
    K: This really strange light yih know, like old fashioned lights?
                                                      (SN 682)

The extension of M's turn was not necessary to elicit a response by K, as can be seen by the fact that K's response to the question overlaps with M's PCE. However, taken in terms of its previous context, the exact target of M's disbelief is, in fact, clarified by the PCE. Without the PCE, the target could have been one of many aspects of the previous report: (1) the lights as the cause of the problem, (2) the fact that the lights made the women look ugly, (3) the fact that the women would not go out, or (4) the fact that the women wanted to sue. As can be seen from K's second turn after M's question, K has heard and is responding to the question of the lights, which M specifically targets through his PCE.

A notable aspect of fragment 15 is that the *because* does not entirely relate to the question, *Are you serious?*. In fact, it makes some unspecified connection to the preceding talk. That is, it relates to some assertion in the discourse previous to the immediate turn: either the fact that the women were suing, or the fact that the light made them look ugly. Thus, the intonational separation of this clause from the previous one is associated with its semantic relatedness to a span of text greater than that previous clause.

Example 16, below, is another case in which a turn could be followed by some kind of response from the listener. C is giving V advice on how to handle her mother. Here C delivers an imperative, ending in final intonation. She then adds on some support for the command, the support introduced by '*cause*.

(16)
    C: Well I wouldn't waste your time- I mean I hate to say this, but
       I wouldn't go- I wouldn't- waste your energy trying to
       convince her;, I ⌈mean=
    V: ⌊Ye:ah.
    C: =if she calls you, you can just say,=
    V: =Ye⌈ah.
    C: ⌊in a very steady way, I think you're wrong

```
         Mom. I think- I'm convinced that it's Okay. But don't put
         your energy, into trying to convince her.
→        ⎡'Cause I-I just think, your gonna be frustrated.
   V:    ⎣Yea:h.                                              (K 361)
```

Again, as in example 15 above, a recipient response overlaps with the turn extension. It would be interesting to know whether a quicker uptake is expected after certain types of speech acts, ones that strongly prefer agreement and clearly designate a particular recipient. While transcribers may not hear pauses in these cases, participants in the conversation may hear an interactional gap, however small. In illustrating the contrast between preferred and dispreferred responses, Levinson (1983, citing Atkinson and Drew 1979) gives an example of a preferred response to an invitation that is delivered "not only without delay, but actually in partial overlap" (1983:334). Wilson and Zimmerman (1986) found interactionally significant gap lengths to be remarkably short, suggesting that conversationalists are much more sensitive to pause duration than was previously believed. Davidson (1984) refers to these points of potential uptake as "monitor spaces," places where the speaker can extend an utterance and cover up emerging disagreement.

A final environment in which an adverbial clause may connect back to an utterance already closed with final intonation, occurs in long turns that involve the description of events or the explanation of outcomes. These cases are the least amenable to interactional accounts for their addition; they seem to be the result of self-editing, rather than the result of recipient prompting. However, in most of these instances, it is not clear whether the extensions are addressing trouble, or whether they simply represent a regular strategy for structuring information. In explaining already stated outcomes, these may be special cases of a type of rhetorical development in which an outcome is first offered, followed by the unpacking, so to speak, of details and background leading to the outcome.

In example 17, the outcome of getting the car painted is reported in an utterance completed with final intonation. What follows is a description of what the character did to arrive at the outcome. The explanatory portion of the talk is introduced by *because*.

(17)
```
      K:   Plus once he got- (0.8) some u:m (1.3) he got some battery
           acid on: (0.2) his trunk or something
           (the⎡t) somebody did.
    (R):      ⎣Ooh I did too
           (0.3)
→     K:   'An he got the whole thing painted. Because he said, (0.3)
           some uh (0.1) gas station attendant, (0.6) had (0.8) screwed
           it up'n:, put some battery acid on his trunk,
```
(SN 445)

This use of a PCE does not seem to be responsive to trouble. *Because* seems to simply be the connector used to introduce the next component of the story. In this case the story has been structured with the background following the report of the outcome.

In the next example, A is trying to explain that most people are not in school on Fridays. She seems to get mixed up in her explanation, and in the end it is not very clear what she is saying. In any case, she uses a conditional PCE, at the arrow:

(18)
```
      B:   I wonder if Do:nna went back to school, iz
           ⎡I was curious to know,
      A:   ⎣I n- Y'know- Fridays is a funny day. mMost a' the
           people in schoo:l, .hh that's why I only have classes on
           Tuesday an' Fri:day, .hh (0.3) u- one cla:ss, because most a'
           them have o:ff those days.
           Yih kno⎡w=
      B:          ⎣Ye::h
→     A:   =like if you could work your schedule out that ⎡way.
      B:                                                   ⎣Right.
```
[TG 662]

The PCE in example 18 is not prompted by the recipient, but seems instead to be a speaker-based attempt to clarify her turn. The outcome of getting off on Tuesdays and Fridays is not what A was able to work out, and the final *if*-clause seems to be trying to make that clear.

In two final examples we will look at in this section, B is talking about the trouble she has been having in finding the textbooks for one of her classes. The PCEs in these examples come as parts of a long stretch of talk in which B has special rights to the floor. The recipient, A, provides appropriate minimal responses to subparts of B's explanation. Both these cases involve self-editing without recipient prompting, with *because* serving as an introducer of background information.

(19)
```
        B: The mo:dern art. The twentieth century a:rt there's about
           eight books,
        A: Mm ⌈ hm,
        B:    ⌊ An' I went to buy a book the other day. I ⌈ went=
        A:                                                ⌊ (mm)
    →   B: =.hh went down to N.Y.U. to get it. Because it's the only place
           that car ⌈ ries the book.
        A:         ⌊ Mmm                                        (TG 306)
```

In example 19, there could be a receipt marker by A after *... to get it*, but instead, B adds on an explanatory causal clause. In fact, the reason for B's going to NYU is not recoverable from the context, and there is good motivation for adding the causal explanation. But while B's talk is sensitive to what her recipient may be expected to know and what she must be told, the PCE itself is not responsive to any evident trouble between A and B. If there is any trouble evident here, it is only internal to B's turn. She is using the causal connection to structure the unfolding information.

Later in the same sequence, B is talking about another book.

(20)
```
        B: So she told me of a place on Madison Avenue 'n Seventy Ninth
           Street.=
        A: =M ⌈ mm.
    →   B:   ⌊ To go an' try the:re. Because I als- I tried
           Barnes 'n Nobles. 'N, (0.6) they didn't have anything they don't
           have any art books she told me.
                                                              [TG 352]
```

In this example, the *because* seems to be introducing a jump back in the sequence of events. In telling the events, B reports the second event first and then fills in the first, introducing it with *because*.

5.2.3 Section summary

In section 5.2, I have reviewed the ways that same speakers may add final adverbial clauses to their own prior turns. Table 14

Table 14. *Types of post-completion extensions*

	Temporal	Conditional	Causal	Concessive	Total
1 Prompted by pause, recipient turn		3	14		17
2 Accounts of dispreferreds			7		7
3 Extensions of first pair parts (NO PROMPT)	3		4		7
4 Self-edit	1	1	9	2	13
Total	4	4	34	2	44[4]

summarizes the types of post-completion extensions found in the corpus, showing the number of cases of each type and the adverbial clause types represented.

As can be seen from Table 14, a majority of the same speaker PCEs in this corpus can be tied to interactional motivations. Types 1–3 (representing 70% of the cases of same speaker extensions), can be understood with respect to the preference structure of conversations, a general tendency to pursue agreement or "coming to an understanding" (Sacks 1987). The PCEs that originate from interaction are prompted by pauses, questions, and even receipt tokens when some other type of response is being pursued, and sometimes forming the account portions of dispreferred responses. In the case of Type 3 PCEs, though no pause is hearable to the transcriber, I have suggested that certain speech acts, i.e., questions and commands, may involve very close monitoring on the part of the speaker for recipient uptake. It may be that a dispreferred response, or even an interactionally significant lapse of time, following such acts is particularly avoided, a circumstance that engenders the rapid addition of PCEs in these environments.

PCEs do also occur where no obvious prompting or other clear

Final adverbial clauses after ending intonation 123

interactional motivation is present. In Type 3 cases (about 30% of the same speaker extensions in the corpus), the final adverbial clauses seem most like what have been referred to as "afterthoughts" in the literature (Chafe 1984). Whereas many adverbial clause PCEs are clearly the products of negotiation between speaker and listener, this last pattern appears to be the product of speaker-based feedback and editing. However, it is still open to question whether these types of extensions can be considered to be added in order to repair what has gone before (i.e., mistakes fixed by afterthrought extensions) or whether they simply represent one manner of structuring the development of discourse: introducing background and elaboration after more general reports have been given.

Table 14 also shows that a great majority of the same speaker adverbial clause PCEs are introduced by causal conjunctions (34 out of 44, 77%). As was pointed out in chapter 4, the preponderance of causals in final position, as well as their preponderance after utterances that have already been treated as possibly complete, suggests that causal conjunctions introduce a different type of information than other adverbial conjunctions. Not only are *because* or *'cause* more likely than other adverbial conjunctions to follow final intonation, that is, the material they introduce is very often intonationally separated from the material being modified or elaborated, but they are also more likely than other adverbial conjunctions to follow pauses or recipient prompts. Thus, the material they introduce is associated with interactional negotiation. The use of causal conjunctions to introduce information addressing interactional trouble is particularly evident in the presentation of the account portion of a dispreferred response. When an adverbial conjunction is used to introduce an account for a dispreferred response, it is always causal. *Because* and *'cause*, then, work as general introducers of background or motivating information, and environments where such information is appropriate are very often environments where a recipient has displayed a need for further elaboration. Temporal and conditional information, though sometimes appearing after prior material has been displayed as complete (intonationally), are much more likely to appear as intonationally coherent with the material they modify, suggesting that these conjunctions introduce material that is more predictably necessary for some information to be clear. Causal conjunctions, in contrast, often do extra work when there has been an interactional warrant for more elaboration.

5.3 Adverbial clause extensions to other speakers' turns

In cases of final adverbial clauses that follow ending intonation, it has been argued that feedback from, and negotiation with, the recipient contributes to the perception of a need for further elaboration or qualification. Thus, final adverbial clauses produced by the same speaker after the previous utterance has been treated as complete are often the products of more than one speaker – the recipient prompting engenders jointly produced extensions of utterances. There is another group of final adverbial clauses that are also joint productions. These are cases in which a recipient adds a final adverbial clause to the previous person's talk. While such collaborative utterances could be produced across continuing intonation, in the present corpus, PCEs by different speakers are produced only after ending intonation on the parts of previous speakers.

Different-speaker PCEs serve three interactional purposes in these conversations: they display agreement or understanding, they check understanding, and they serve as vehicles for co-telling when more than one speaker is explaining, reporting, or telling the same story.[5]

A recipient may signal that s/he is listening to a speaker by providing minimal receipt tokens at appropriate points in a speaker's talk. Thus, in the following example, C displays that she is listening by providing the receipt marker, *mm hm*:

(21)
    K: It was like the other day uh,
        (0.2)
    Vera (.) was talking on the phone to her *mom*?
→   C: Mm hm.   (K 1–5)

Such a response shows that the recipient is listening, but it does not *display* understanding of the content of the previous talk.

A recipient may provide more than a minimal receipt marker and, in so doing, display understanding rather than merely indicating attention. In the next example, C and V both display more than a minimal hearing by providing more than minimal responses.

(22)
```
35  V:  Okay, this is what th-the problem is. My dad's knee-
36      leg was very bowlegged. It was like (.)
37      thirt⎡een degrees,
38  C:       ⎣All his life. (.) Right?
39  V:  Well:, more in old age(h).=
40  C:  =Uh huh.
41      (0.5)
42  V:  s-Slightly anyways. Ve⎡ry weak knees.
43  C:                        ⎣Yeah yeah, I remember
44      noticing that. You- (.) y- y- he's- uh- he's had it
        for awhile.=
46  V:  =Oh yeah. Ever since I can remember. hh    (K 35–45)
```

At line 43, C claims understanding and recognition first through the receipt tokens *Yeah yeah* that overlap with V's talk, and then through the added statement that she remembers noticing V's father's bowleggedness. While the receipt tokens claim a hearing and possible understanding or recognition of V's report, the claim that C then adds upgrades her claim of understanding.

At line 46, we find V responding to C's indirect question, *he's had it for awhile*. V provides a token of strong agreement, *Oh yeah*, and then she adds a display of agreement showing her interpretation of C's *awhile*. Here, then, we see an adverbial clause, connected back to another speaker's talk, used as part of a response to the previous speaker's talk. C's *awhile* being interpreted, qualified, and perhaps even corrected by V's temporal clause, *ever since I can remember*. The adverbial clause structure is exploited in interactional work across speakers.

In the next example, H and N are making plans to get together in the evening. H uses a conditional clause with no main clause to make an offer. N accepts and uses a causal clause to display her understanding of why the offer is appropriate.

(23)
```
        N:  So it starts at eight thir⎡ty?
        H:                             ⎣.hh Yeah.So, if I- k-
            pick you up li:ke by eight o'clo::⎡ck,
        N:                                    ⎣Yeah. She said-
     →      (0.2) Well 'cause I'm so clo:se. Too.
        H:  Yeah,                                    (HG 14.1)
```

The *'cause* plus the marker *too* both signal that the clause should connect back to previous talk. In this case, N provides reasoning that supports H's offer to pick N up and, thus, displays agreement.[6]

An adverbial clause that connects back to a previous speaker's talk need not be preceded by a receipt token; the grammatical connection itself can be a display of agreement. In the next example, H is reporting on a troubled relationship she has with a man.

(24)
```
        H:  I know it's (.) playing games'n every ⌈thi:ng but
  →     N:                                        ⌊Y e a h but
            you want him to, (.) ⌈write first.
  →     H:                       ⌊.hhhhhhhhh 'cause I really feel
            that, it was sincere enough, where he(w)- WOULD of.=
        N:  =Ye:ah.                                          (HG 29.25)
```

At the first arrow, N shows her understanding by collaborating with H's talk; N agrees (*Yeah*) and characterizes what H wants (*him to write first.*). H then adds a causal clause to N's talk. By adding the causal clause, H incorporates N's talk into her own, and thus displays her acceptance of N's interpretation.

Similarly, in the next example, J shows his understanding and agreement with P by adding on a final adverbial. P's roommates are out for the night, and P doesn't want to be bothered by them when they get home.

(25)
```
        P:  I've got the apartment to myself, and I'm gonna take advantage
            of it goin to bed early.
        J:  Oh⌈:::
        P:    ⌊N' they come home, they gonna talk about it. And
            I'm gonna go to be::d.=
  →     J:  =Before they get there, yeah,                     (PJ 11.1)
```

Notice here that although an agreement token does not precede the adverbial clause, one does follow it. In this case, rather than providing an adverbial clause to support a receipt marker, the adverbial clause is given first and the receipt marker signals that the adverbial clause is to be taken as a display of agreement.

Recipients also use adverbial clauses to check their understanding of a prior speaker's talk. In example 26, K has been talking about some women who wanted to sue a city because the street lights made the women look ugly.

(26)
    K: An' they wanted t'sue:.
→   S: 'Cause it hurts business?   (SN 673)

In S's turn, she checks her understanding by using a causal clause connected back to K's previous utterance. In conversation analytic terms, S's turn would be characterized as a "candidate understanding."

Similarly, in example 27, C checks her understanding by connecting a conditional clause to V's talk.

(27)
    V: If he: (0.5) didn't wanna keep being active, an' do sports n' things, right now, at his age, an' with the ba:d condition of his knee, they normally put in a plastic knee.
        (0.2)
    V: A whol:e kn⌈ee replacement.
→   C: ⌊If he didn't wanna be active.   (K 83)

A final way in which adverbial clauses are added on by different speakers involves the sharing of an explanation. In such cases, there is at least one person for whom the information is new, but more than one person is in a position to be able to give the information. The result is that the two or more parties that have access to the information collaborate in telling it.

In example 28, D has been talking about the difference between the way that foreigners and Nepalis react to the health conditions in Kathmandu. At this point in the conversation, W is in the role of recipient, while C and H, both of whom have lived in Nepal, are trying to participate in the telling.

(28)
    D: They don't like the taste of boiled water, y'know, they ya offer 'em boiled water, (Ah.)
    W: ⌈The ta- what ta-?
    D: ⌊There's no ta- there's no ta:ste to it.=
→   H: =Because it gets flat.=
    D: =Yeah.=
    C: =It doesn't (have all that junk in) it, y'know?   (AM 256)

At the arrow, H adds a causal explanation to D's previous talk. D accepts H's co-telling with his agreement token, *yeah*, and at the same time, his agreement reaffirms his role as the main teller or the authority on the subject.[7]

In the next two examples, V and K, girlfriend and boyfriend, collaborate in explaining to the recipient, C, knowledge which V and K share. In the first instance, example 29, C suggests that K doesn't have the same kind of family as V and C do, so he doesn't understand how they react to their families. Both V and K object to this characterization, with V adding support to K through a final causal, at the arrow.

(29)
```
    C: Your parents are just too normal Kip. You don't understa:nd
       what it's like to have weird parents.=
    K: =Oh I have a grandmother
       ⌈that makes me understand⌈Vera's mom a lot so,
    V: ⌊He has a grandmother th  │at's like my mom.
    C:                            ⌊Oh.
    C: Uh huh .hh
    V: He does.
    C: I mean that- the- but ya know ya don't understand how Vera
       could be so affected. I think about my
       ⌈dad °ya know.
    K: ⌊(           )⌈I understan-
    V:               ⌊ I get sucked in.
    K: I understand.
    C: Yeah?
    K: But I-I don't unde⌈r-
→   V:                   ⌊'Cause his mo:m gets sucked i⌈n.
    C:                                                  ⌊O::h.
    V: Doesn't she?
    K: Yeah.                                                  (K 245)
```

Notice that V defers to K as the authority on this issue. She asks *Doesn't she?* to establish that her collaboration with K has been appropriate.

The second time they collaborate with an adverbial clause, K uses a causal clause, connected back to V's talk, to explain why V is upset about her father's condition.

(30)
```
    V: I said are you s(h)ur:e this is gonna make him more
       comfortable. I mean what⌈is the-
    C:                          ⌊What?
          (0.2)
```

Final adverbial clauses after ending intonation 129

```
      V:  The surgery.=
      C:  =But it's already done anyway, isn't it?
      V:  Oh it's done, but I-⎡I was so-⎡  upse:t. I w-
      C:             ⎣Oh.   ⎣Yeah uh huh
→     K:  'Cause he's in a lot of pain. Right n⎡ow.
      C:                  ⎢Yeah.
      V:                  ⎣Ya know.        (K 301)
```

We can see, then, that adverbial clauses are one convenient way in which speakers can display agreement (n = 5) or check understanding of prior utterances (n = 2). Adverbial clauses may also serve as a vehicle whereby a speaker can move to co-tell some piece of information (n = 3).

Table 15. *Adverbial clause extensions to other speakers' turns*

Understanding display	Understanding check	Sharing explanation	Total
5	2	3	10

Whether an adverbial clause is used to display agreement, check understanding, or co-tell, it is an efficient strategy in that it makes use of, and incorporates, another person's talk. In fact, it is, at least in part, this coordination with another speaker's talk that makes adverbial clauses particularly effective in signaling understanding of both the content and form of prior talk.

5.4 Summary

In this chapter, we have looked at adverbial clauses that appear after final intonation, either added by the same speaker or by another speaker. The interactional circumstances from which such post-completion extensions (PCEs) arise are quite different from the environments of adverbial clauses that are intonationally coherent with their main clauses. In a majority of cases adverbial clauses that follow final intonation arise from interactionally significant circumstances which are best understood by reference to the preference structure of ordinary conversation, the tendency for interactional negotiation of agreement. PCEs may be prompted either by a recipient response or by an obvious gap, a perceptible pause in the interaction at a point where a response would be appropriate. There are also contexts in which, even in the absence of either a pause or a dispreferred response from the recipient, a speaker may add a PCE to help avoid any obvious sign of interactional trouble. PCEs may also form the account portions of dispreferred or non-agreeing turns.

The interactional motivation for PCEs is particularly clear in cases of adverbial clauses added by a next speaker to a prior speaker's talk. In such cases, speakers make interactional use of adverbial clauses in order to check understanding, display agreement, and collaborate in reports or stories.

It is clear, then, that in conversation, as opposed to written or spoken monologue, what have been conceived of as "afterthoughts," products of single speaker cognitive processes, must, in a majority of instances, be considered joint productions emerging through interactional negotiation.

6

Comparison of clause types and apparent deviations from the general patterns

In the preceding chapters, I have explored the work that adverbial clauses do in conversation, and in what positions they do that work. In addition to the usage patterns focused upon in chapters 3–5, there is interesting variation in the distribution and functions of the three major types of adverbial clauses found in the corpus. In the present chapter, I compare the placement and functions of the different clause types, and I also highlight some apparent violations of the general principles discussed in previous chapters. The exceptions serve to further elucidate the principles themselves.

6.1 Different clause types in initial versus final placement

Examining variation in the use of different clause types, we find that causal clauses, while not appearing initially, do frequently appear in final position after continuing intonation. In final position, causal clauses do work that is distinct from the work of other final adverbial clauses. These differences are consistent with the semantics of the different clause types, causals presenting explanatory or motivating material, rather than temporal or situational grounding.

As can be seen from Figure 1, of all temporal clauses, most (52.5%) appear finally after continuing intonation. That is, a majority of temporal clauses in this corpus are being used to complete main clause meaning, rather than to structure the discourse (or add more material after an utterance is finished – to be discussed in section 6.2). Utterances in these conversations, then, seem to be regularly provided with some temporal or situational grounding through temporal clauses. In a portion of these cases,

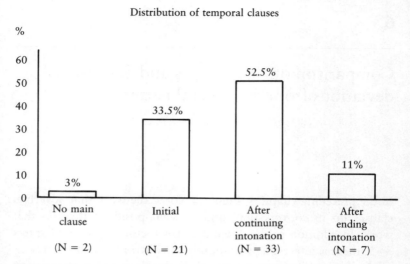

Figure 1. How are temporal clauses distributed in relation to main clauses?

the temporal clause is used initially and thus does double duty, specifying a time or situation, and at the same time organizing the talk around a temporal frame. But in a majority of instances, temporal grounding is done in final position, and the temporal clause is not selected as the point of departure for a unit of talk. The use of initial position for temporal clauses seems to be reserved for points in the development of an event sequence when a highlighted, or more crucial, event is to be presented.

On the other hand, conditionals are much less common in final position after continuing intonation (23%) than they are in initial position (see Figure 2). When conditional clauses are used, they are most commonly used initially. Conditional clauses seem, then, to be prototypically textual in their functioning. Haiman (1978) was the first to argue for a relationship between conditionals and topics. He found that a number of languages mark both conditional prostases and sentence topics with the same morphemes. The overwhelming use of conditional clauses in initial position, serving as frameworks for the interpretation of propositions that follow, is very much in concurrence with the proposed functional

General patterns and apparent deviations

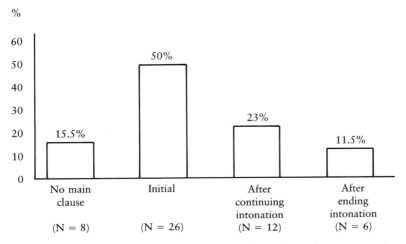

Figure 2. How are conditional clauses distributed in relation to main clauses?

similarity of conditional prostases and topics. Thus, the distribution and function of *if*-clauses in the present English conversational corpus offers further discourse-based support (along with work by Ford and Thompson 1986) for the association first observed by Haiman, based on sentence-level data.

Why should the distribution of conditional qualification be so skewed toward initial position, the position associated with interclausal linkage and discourse organization? I would suggest that the use of *if*-clauses in initial position has to do with the fact that their meaning lends itself inherently to discourse organizational work. *If*-clauses, at the content level alone, function primarily to limit the framework of interpretation for an associated main clause. That is, the primary function of conditional clauses is the creation of temporary discourse realities; they provide text-created realities in the context of which associated propositions may be accepted as real. The use of conditional clauses has to do with the organization of ideas in a world created by the unfolding discourse, rather than the representation of real states or events. The fact that conditional clauses have this essentially discourse

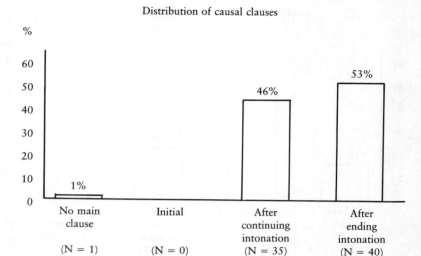

Figure 3. How are causal clauses distributed in relation to main clauses?

function, even when viewed semantically alone, may well be related to their predominance in initial position, where discourse level linkage and organizational work is most regularly attended to in English.[1]

What we see, then, in comparing initial and final adverbial clauses, is that there is a more diverse set of contexts for the occurrence of final adverbial clauses, and a more limited set of discourse functions for initial adverbial clauses. Final adverbial clauses specify main clause meaning, but do not participate in information patterning strategies as do initial adverbials. In line with previous studies of adverbial clause placement, final adverbial clauses, in these conversations, have a "local semantic function" (Thompson 1985b:69). And initial adverbial clauses may be characterized as playing a "broader discourse role" (Thompson 1985b:69). Temporal clauses are very common in final position, as are causals, which, in contrast, do not appear initially. And conditionals occur finally much less frequently than they do initially, which supports the notion that conditional clauses are prototypically discourse linking and framing in their use – as has

General patterns and apparent deviations 135

been suggested through the comparisons of conditional clauses to discourse topics.

6.2 Different clause types as new intonation units

One striking observation with regard to post-completion extensions in this corpus is that they are overwhelmingly causal, introduced by *because* or *'cause*. Out of a total of 55 adverbial clauses following final intonation, 40 or 73% are causal.

Viewed in terms of the distribution of each clause type (Figures 1–3, pp. 132–134), of all causal adverbial clauses, 53% (n = 40) follow final intonation (Figure 3). In contrast, the proportion of all conditional clauses in this pattern is only 11.5%, and of temporals only 11%.

Why should causal adverbial extensions be so common after previous units have been presented as possibly complete? As is the case for conditionals, which dominate initial position, the semantics of causals, i.e., the type of information they usually introduce, is well-suited for placement after the units they modify. *Because* and *'cause* introduce background, support, sources, and motivation for associated material. In fact, some cases of *because* might be paraphrased as "what I have just said may be clarified through what I am about to say."[2] Causal conjunctions, then, become broadly useful for introducing material in response to interactional trouble. They target what has just been said as needing elaboration, and they then provide the elaboration. Conditional and temporal conjunctions are more limited semantically, conditionals involving hypotheticality and temporals dealing with time, whereas *because* and *'cause* make a commitment only to present clarifying material – with very little constraint on the nature of that material. This broad range of possible content makes causal conjunctions well-adapted to use after the possible ends of utterances, where interactional trouble may appear and recipient responses, or lack thereof, may prompt extensions. In such circumstances, extensions done with causal conjunctions may generally add background, detail, explanation, or other elaboration. Temporal and conditional clauses are most often presented in continuous intonation contours with the material they modify, whether they appear initially or finally. They are much less often used as vehicles for the extension of utterances with the goal of further clarification of a preceding unit which has been closed intonationally.

6.3 *If*-clauses without main clauses

A discussion of the differences in the use of temporal, conditional, and causal clauses in the corpus would not be complete without some attention to the conditional clauses that stand alone without main clauses. While many of these pattern like initial adverbial clauses as discussed in chapter 3, there is a special interactional use of *if*-clauses that should be noted.

Before I focus on the special uses of *if*-clauses, let me provide a picture of how adverbial clauses may be used without main clauses when the main clause meaning is recoverable from the context. The corpus contains a small number (n = 11) of adverbial clauses, i.e., clauses introduced by adverbial conjunctions, that do not have identifiable main clauses. Among these are adverbial clauses whose main clauses may be easily filled in from the context. Speakers seem to be operating on the principle of least effort. Thus, in the following example, V has been reporting on one nurse's reassurances about V's father's expected recovery from his knee operation:

```
(1) (she refers to the nurse)
    V: But it was s-so: upsetting that I- an' I needed to straighten it
       out in my own ⌈head.
    C:              ⌊.hh and
       he is healing. I mean it's a little
       abnor⌈rmal but basical ⌈ly
    V:    ⌊Yes:            ⌊He's- he's had a little
       problem,
    C: R-uh hu⌈h.
    V:        ⌊Ya know other than the regular. hh But
       it is healing, n' she said we've seen it over an'
       over an- an' they get better.
    C: Mm hm.
    V: ⌈No
    C: ⌊How fast?
       (0.2)
    V: Three months.
       (0.3)
```

General patterns and apparent deviations

```
        C: °M ⌈m hm
        V:    ⌊Three months of- of crutches.
        C: Mm hm.
           (0.3)
        V: But chyou know (0.3) Anyway she said it's gonna be better,
           he's gonna feel better, his knee's not gonna hurt, we've seen it
           over an' over.
           =An'⌈I kept=
        K:    ⌊( )
        V: =a:sking her ya know are you su⌈:re,
        C:                                ⌊Right right.
        V: She said well w- ya know she didn't say yes your dad,
        C: Yeah.
→       V: will but she said when you see hi:m n',
           (0.2)
        C: Mm hm.
        V: .hh so I- what I wanna do with my mom is go back to her n'-
           tell her ya know I checked this ou:t, an' I'm convinced.
                                                                    (K 340)
```

As can be seen from the talk that precedes the incomplete temporal clause (at the arrow), the content of any associated main clause is entirely predictable. Having already extensively listed the nature of the nurse's reassurances, V can assume the recipients will not need her to complete her initial *when*-clause at the arrow.

Similarly, in the next example, R is speculating on the possible outcome of his submission of a script to a television studio. He states and evaluates one possibility through a conditional clause plus a main clause, and he then explores the contrasting option. However, the second main clause is not delivered:

(2)
```
        A: Of course they might say (0.2) uhm: (0.3)
           this is go:od,
           (0.5)
        A: Do ya have another one.=
        R: =.hhh If they say tha:t (0.2) the:n (.)
           I'm home free.
           (0.4)
        R: Then I'm happy.
        A: Yeah,
→       R: If they sa:y, I'm sorry this is so:: ba:d, (.) I dunno know what
           t the f- ⌈(0.2) what:t (was in your head,)
        A:         ⌊Whh .hheh heh ha ha
        A: .hhh but Cliff likes i:t,                        (AR 163)
```

In the context, the incomplete clause complex is not treated as a problem.

The cases in examples 1 and 2 involve adverbial clauses as parts of longer rhetorical units which render the potential main clauses easily predictable. Within their discourse contexts, such cases pattern like initial adverbial clauses and were included in the discussion of initial adverbial clauses in chapter 3. In contrast with those, which could be termed cases of "ellipted" main clauses, there are several cases in which the adverbial clauses seem to be functioning entirely autonomously. These cases, while few in number, are worth noting as they seem quite acceptable and familiar and yet do not find mention in leading grammars that endeavor to cover spoken English usage (Leech and Svartvik 1975, Celce-Murcia and Larsen-Freeman 1983, Quirk, Greenbaum, Leech, and Svartvik 1985).

Basically, these are *if*-clauses that make offers:

(3)
```
A: But if you wanna-uh:m (0.2) come in, en' s'see.
B: Tch! I wouldn't know where to look for her(hh)
   hnhh-hnh⌈h .hh
A:         ⌊Well you know, you know, come along with
            me,                                    (TG 665)
```

(4)
```
A: Well if you want me (to) give you a ring tomorrow morning.
B: Tch! .hhh We:ll y-you know, let's, eh-j I don't know, I'll see
   (h) maybe I won't even be in,                   (TG 739)
```

(5) (About a play the two speakers plan to attend)
```
N: So it starts at eight thir⌈ty?
H:                            ⌊.hh Yeah. So, if I- K-
   pick you up li:ke by eight o'clo::⌈ck,
N:                                    ⌊Yeah,
                                               (HG 13.25)
```

In these cases, the recipients either disagree (as in examples 3 and 4) or agree (as in example 5), but in any case, they treat the autonomous adverbial clauses as complete conversational actions in themselves. *If*-clauses are chosen here as the vehicles for offers or for reinforcing offers that have already been made. Conditional clauses are good candidates for use in this independent manner because, in their discourse contexts, they most often encode options. The opposing option or options are either explicitly

General patterns and apparent deviations 139

stated or are implicit. Thus, when one makes an offer, a speech act which proposes that another person participate in the plan of action one is proposing, an *if*-clause is a workable format for suggesting the plan of action and at the same time displaying a recognition, or conceding to the fact, that the plan is contingent and the other party may prefer another option.[3] Thus, the optionality associated with *if*-clauses in their most common usage in this corpus makes *if*-clauses useful formats for offers. These autonomous *if*-clauses working as offers, or to reinforce offers, represent another way in which conditional clause usage differs from the use of temporal and causal clauses.

6.4 Apparent deviations from the patterns

In sections 6.1 through 6.3, I reviewed the general distribution of the different adverbial clause types in this corpus, proposing some functional motivations for those patterns. In this section, I will look at some of the instances of clause placement that seem to go against the general trends. I will use the discussion of exceptions as an opportunity to clarify the kinds of jobs that get done in each of the positions that adverbial clauses take relative to their associated modified material: initial, final after continuing intonation, and final after possibly complete utterances. Clause types were differentially distributed between the three placement options. Of all conditional clauses, a majority occurred in initial position doing discourse organizational work (Figure 2). Of all temporal clauses, a majority occurred finally after continuing intonation, completing the main clause meaning (Figure 1). Causal clauses were divided between the two final positions, after continuing and after ending intonation; but causals were absent in initial position (Figure 3).

I would like to examine first two cases of temporal clauses that come neither before their main clauses, where 33.5% of all temporals appear, nor after continuing intonation, where 52.5% of all temporals appear. Rather than being connected intonationally to their main clauses, as are most temporal clauses, these are among the very few temporal clauses (n = 7, 11%) that occur after the previous clause has terminated in final intonation. Thus, while the general tendency is for the intonation to tie together temporal clauses and their main clauses, the intonation in these cases shows a separation; so, whereas a principle seems to be operating whereby temporal modification is more closely tied to the material it modifies, in these cases, the connection is looser. These cases, then, give us a chance to observe the circumstances in which a clause type containing temporal information might be separated from its main clause.

The first case involves a speaker who has problems in the middle of his utterance. The turn represents C's contribution to a sequence in which the participants are commenting on characters from a story M has just told. A man named Keegan was one of the main characters in M's story. Where this fragment begins, G is finishing a story about another member of the Keegan family.

(6) (simplified)
```
     G:  Went home after work from then on I guess,
     M:  Mhhhhmmhhmmmmm
     C:  He::h heh heh heh-eh heh
     M:  °hheh hh
     C:  Keegan used to race uhr uh- er it was um, (0.4) used to run um
         (3.7)
     C:  Oh:: shit.
         (0.4)
     C:  Uhm,
         (0.4)
     C:  Fisher's car.
     M:  Three an'⎡a quarter?
     C:        ⎣Three an' a quarter.
  →  M:  Yeh,
         (1.0)
  →  C:  When I was foolin' around.
     G:  I used to go over there with my cousin (when he had a car),
                                                        (AD 17.19)
```

In the first place, this final *when*-clause has good reason for being disconnected from its main clause, because the search for a correct name for the car intervenes, a search that involves participation from M. C's turn is opened up in the middle, and an interactional sequence is inserted. C shows he is having trouble through the pauses and *Oh shit*. He gives a hint with *Fisher's car*. Finally, M supplies the appropriate term, with C overlapping M's suggestion with a collaborative completion. It is after this turn-internal interactional sequence that the final *when*-clause is added.

General patterns and apparent deviations 141

But why would C feel the need to add this clause after so much else has intervened? The importance of the temporal reference has to do with the fact that it provides a justification for C's making this particular comment at this point in the talk. In the general context, each of the men is telling about a personal connection he has to car racing or to the characters in the story. Just to name the kind of car that Keegan drove would not fit into the type of talk being done here. After M provides a confirmation of the type of car (*Yeh*, first arrow), a pause follows. The pause is a sign that C's turn may not have provided a clear direction for further talk; notice that C has not shown the relevance of his turn to the topic at hand. C then adds the temporal clause through which he shows his own personal connection with the race track. G's turn, just following C's *when*-clause, is another of the same type: a telling that shows G's personal connection to the race track. And the story that G is finishing at the beginning of this fragment told of G's personal experience with a relative of Keegan's who works with G. In such a sequential context, then, there is good reason for C to add the *when*-clause PCE to show his personal connection.

In example 6, then, a temporal clause appears in an uncommon environment for such a clause. It does so in part because of a repair sequence that comes in the middle of the utterance, and in part because the temporal clause itself is crucial for showing the relevance of C's turn to its sequential context. There is a compelling motivation, then, for this exception to the general pattern that temporal clauses are connected to their main clauses across continuing intonation boundaries.

In another case of a final temporal after final intonation, G, in the following fragment, extends his request with a *while*-clause:

(7)
    G: Bartender? How about a beer.   While your settin' there.
                                                                                   (AD 11.22)

The person of whom G is making the request, in fact the host of the picnic, is closer to the beer than G, and G presents this fact as a reason for the request. So, even though the extension is in the form of a temporal clause, what the clause contributes cannot be considered to be temporal grounding alone. The added clause is justifying the request. Example 7 involves another instance of a clause type appearing in a less common position for good reason:

this clause is doing a different kind of job than temporal clauses generally do.

Moving to another clause type, there is one last case of interest in terms of its potential violation of a very general tendency. This instance involves the only environment where potentially initial causals appear. As has been extensively discussed here, causals are exclusively final in this corpus, and this fragment contains the only cases that could be seen as departing from that pattern. Causal clauses generally present background or motivation in interactional moves that are responsive to perceptible problems in the talk. There seems to be very little occasion, in this corpus, for causal clauses to be used in a discourse orientational function in initial position. As suggested in chapter 4, one reason for the lack of this function for causal clauses may have to do with the greater complexity of causal associations. This means that a greater degree of planning may be called for in order for causal clauses to be used as pivotal points in the development of discourse.

In the light of the possibility of a cognitive constraint that works against the use of causal clauses in initial position in spontaneous interaction, the context for the potentially initial clauses in this fragment is worth examining. The information that appears in both of these clauses is present, almost in its entirety, in the preceding context. Thus, very little cognitive effort is necessary to construct these clauses.

In example 8, V is explaining the possible operations that her father's doctors considered:

(8)
```
     V : This side of the cartilage, wa- b-being worn (it-) ga-gone. in
         his kne⎡e, an' it was swelling .hh
     C :      ⎣Mm
     V : So the doctors said, that they would- (0.3) If he: (0.5) didn't
         wanna keep being active, an' do sports n' things, right now, at
         his age, an' with the bad condition of his knee, they normally
         put in a plastic knee.
                 (0.2)
     V : A whol:e kn⎡ee replacement.
     C :            ⎣If he didn't wanna be active but
→            ⎡since he wa:nted to be active,
       V :   ⎣If he didn't want to.
→      V : Since my dad wants to⎡con
       C :                       ⎣I can imagine your dad saying
```

General patterns and apparent deviations 143

```
              no no, that's alright, I won't be active.
→   V :       Oh⎡no no no. He wouldn't do that.=
    K :        ⎣Huh huh huh
→   V :     =cause he wants to continue ski:ing⎡n' stuff.
    C :                                        ⎣right
    V :     So they said okay in that case, (0.2) we will cut a we:dge out,
            (0.5) and straighten the leg.                              (K 76)
```

The context for C's potentially initial causal (first arrow) is after the polar opposite has appeared twice: once in V's turn, *If he didn't wanna keep being active . . .*, and once in C's repeat of V's talk, *If he didn't wanna be active.*

V's *since*-clause (second arrow) is the beginning of a paraphrase of C's *since*-clause. V's *since my dad wants to con-* can be analyzed as having the same content as *he wanted to be active* when we see it completed a few lines later as, *cause he wants to continue skiing n stuff*, meaning, of course, he wants to be active. Again, then, we see that violations of the general tendencies found in the data occur in very special circumstances, for reasons that clearly distinguish them from the typical cases. In this fragment, causals are potentially able to appear in a discourse organizational position precisely because so little cognitive effort is needed to form their content.[4]

What needs further discussion in this example is the fact that after appearing in possible initial clauses two times, the same content appears in a post-completion extension, *Cause he wants to continue skiing n stuff* (fourth arrow). This occurrence shows very nicely that even when one can establish that some information is cognitively accessible by the fact that it appears in preceding discourse, this does not *determine* that the information must be used rhetorically or interactionally in a position that reflects its accessibility. In example 8, information that is maximally accessible in the prior context appears in what could be viewed as a maximally unplanned, "afterthought" position (Chafe 1984). Cognitive accessibility of information seems to facilitate the use of initial position in the case of the two *since*-clauses, but in the case of the final *because*-clause, the opportunity provided by cognitive accessibility is not used.

V places the causal information in an interactionally appropriate location. We know that V has already tried to insert a form of this clause into the talk just prior to the *because*-clause, but she is cut off by C (*Since my dad wants to con-*). V is simply using her negative response to C's turn, at the third arrow, as a place to add the same information she was cut off in saying before. The format that is used is one in which a final causal clause forms the account portion of a dispreferred response (discussed in 5.2.1). Thus, information that might be very cognitively accessible is, for interactional reasons, presented in a pattern that might be associated with less accessible information. The contribution of cognitive constraints to the structuring of talk in interaction is clearly just that, a contribution. Cognitive constraints represent parts of a total process that also involves the appropriate fitting of one's utterances into their sequential context.

6.6 Summary

In this chapter I have made explicit comparisons between the work that different adverbial clause types do. Each of the main clause types has a different distribution with respect to the three positions. Conditional clauses are predominantly used in discourse organizational initial position. Conditionals are essentially used for the manipulation of frames of reference, and that semantic function is reflected in the fact that their most common position is initial. Temporals appear commonly in both initial position and in final position after continuing intonation, predominating in the latter position. Temporal information is regularly included after main clauses in order to locate an event, action, or state with reference to other events, actions, or states being talked about. Temporal information can also be placed in initial position to structure a piece of talk around shifts in time or situation. Finally, causal clauses, though absent in initial position, are very common in the two final positions. Most notably, they are far and away the most common adverbial clause type to follow utterances completed with final intonation. Final position, where such a large portion of causals appear, is associated with speaker–recipient negotiation and the extension of turns in the pursuit of agreement or common understanding.

In the last part of this chapter, I explicated several examples which seemed, at first glance, to go against the general patterns of placement of the different clause types. The discussion was presented with the aim of elucidating the distributional and functional findings of this study. I demonstrated that special interactional circumstances can create what appear to be violations of the general patterns, but that, in fact, the exceptions prove the rules. Finally, I suggested that, though cognitive constraints may influence adverbial clause usage, as in the case of the lack of the use of causals in initial position, cognitive accessibility of information does not determine the use of that information in ways that reflect that accessibility.

7

Conclusion

7.1 Summary

In this study, I have used the framework of conversation analysis, and the body of findings associated with that approach, to examine the distribution and functions of temporal, conditional, and causal adverbial clauses in a corpus of American English conversation. In the present corpus, in line with findings from prior text-based analyses, discourse-structuring functions are realized through initial adverbial clauses, while final adverbial clauses tend to work more locally in narrowing main clause meaning without creating links or shift points in a larger discourse pattern. I have suggested that the pattern whereby conditional clauses are most likely to be initial, and causal clauses final, is related to an interaction between the inherent meanings of these clauses and the discourse functions those meanings are particularly suitable for serving. The common discourse organizational use of *if*-clauses is likely related to their hypothetical meaning; they are used to create temporary discourse realities, introducing and forming the background for associated modified material. Causal clauses, which present the sources and precipitating states or events that explain other states or events, are well-suited for appearing after the proposition, to be expanded upon, and for introducing background elaboration. They are especially useful as the vehicles for further explanation when problems arise in interaction. Temporal clauses are used most often in post-verbal position, functioning to ground the situation represented by the verb in time. When temporal clauses are placed initially, they are commonly involved in the structuring of discourse involving sequenced events. Temporal clauses are least common after the preceding clause has been finished with ending intonation. It seems that the fact that final temporal clauses are more likely than other clauses to be intonationally tied to their preceding material is related to a principle whereby temporal grounding, be it by verb morphology or by full temporal clauses, is more communicatively and cognitively essential than conditional or causal modification.[1]

In addition to generally supporting prior monologue-based findings on the functions of initial and final adverbial clauses in English discourse, the present study, through a close analysis of the conversational contexts of adverbial clause usage, provides an enriched understanding of the interactional uses of adverbial clauses. This enriched understanding is founded on the methodological principles and empirical findings available in the discipline of conversation analysis.

In conversation, when an initial temporal clause marks the beginning of a narrative, other participants modify their talk in order to accommodate a longer turn by the story-teller. A temporal clause can also signal the arrival of a high point in the development of a narrative. In such an instance, the listener not only understands the information, but also is alerted to the possible appropriateness of providing a response signaling that he or she is following the development of the story or noting that the story is ending. The completion of a story also has implications for the return to turn-by-turn talk. Thus, not only do initial temporal clauses structure information, they also provide important signals for the smooth operation of the turn-taking system.

Initial conditional clauses presenting options may serve as vehicles for contingent offers, and may also introduce delicate information in a backgrounded or softened manner. The interactionally significant use of conditional clauses to present offers occurs in the absence of main clauses as well. Initial placement of conditional clauses can have interactional motivation when there is a need to avoid reaching possible completion points, a point of possible turn exchange, before a full intended contingency has been presented.

Attention to the operation of the turn-taking elucidates the distribution of temporal and conditional clauses in initial versus final position. Extended spans of talk, in which a speaker has negotiated special rights to the floor, are the most frequent locations in these data for the use of adverbial clauses in initial position. In these more monologic portions of the conversations, more opportunities arise for the discourse organizational function of initial adverbial clauses. Thus, consideration of conversational context is essential for understanding adverbial clause placement.

Interactional considerations also figure strongly in the cases of adverbial clauses following final intonation. Such clauses are very commonly responsive to understanding or agreement problems between speaker and recipient. Problems in understanding and agreement may be signaled by overt prompting or by gaps in talk, perceptible pauses in certain environments being clear indications of interactional trouble. Adverbial clauses added after final intonation are also found to constitute extensions of turns in order to account for disagreement. Whether functioning as extensions of dispreferred responses, or whether occasioned by recipient pauses or prompts, adverbial clauses added after final intonation are best understood in terms of their interactional emergence. A final way in which adverbial clauses are added to already completed utterances is when a recipient uses this syntactically dependent structure as a vehicle for collaboration with another speaker; such cases are invariably associated with interactional motivations.

What we see, then, in the general picture of adverbial clause usage in conversation, is a range of functions that are specifically emergent from the demands on conversational interaction. In language jointly produced by more than one individual, speakers not only organize the presentation of information, but, as part of their work and their motivation for producing talk, they manage their roles in the ongoing interaction. This interactional work is associated with a richly varied significance for the use of grammatical structures such as adverbial clauses. Without a consideration of the way interaction is done, we would have an impoverished understanding of adverbial clause usage in the present corpus.

7.2 This study in relation to other areas of research

There are several areas to which the present research is relevant, including both applied and general linguistics. It is becoming more

Conclusion

and more widely recognized in language pedagogy that our assumptions about the grammar of a language cannot be based exclusively on idealized sentence-level descriptions, derived from native speaker intuitions alone. Celce-Murcia and Larsen-Freeman (1983), in their grammar text for ESL/EFL teachers, support the use of discourse- and data-based research in the following way:

> Since it is commonplace these days to acknowledge that the acquisition of a language involves more than the acquisition of forms and meanings of structures – it involves learning how to use these structures within contexts – we have examined certain structures such as articles and passive voice from a discourse perspective... In other areas we have drawn on insights derived from usage studies designed to determine in what discourse contexts native speakers prefer one form over another.
>
> (1983:v)

The results of the present study add to a growing body of research findings that should serve as resources for ESL/EFL professionals, who now recognize the need for empirically grounded information on grammar from a discourse perspective and with reference to situated usage.

Current linguistic research comparing the differences among genres of English should also be informed by the present findings. In particular, the present findings are relevant to work such as that of Biber (1986), which uses common functions associated with grammatical structures as a basis for conclusions regarding the different functions of language in various domains of language use. The results of the present study indicate that there are special characteristics of conversational language use that make generalizations based on other genres questionable. First of all, the fact that differences in the frequency of initial placement of adverbial clauses are associated with the operation of the turn-taking system suggests that one cannot claim that conversation represents one homogeneous type of language use – the frequency of initial adverbial clause usage must be interpreted with reference to the types of turns being taken by speakers at a given point in a given conversation. Secondly, the fact that *because* functions so commonly to introduce new intonation units in conversation must be considered when one compares causal adverbial clause usage in spoken and written genres. It is likely that certain types of causal clause usage never occur in planned and edited writing; the final causal clauses that follow pauses or listener prompts would have no basis for emergence in formal written English.

Finally, and most fundamentally, studies such as the present one are necessary in order to expand our general understanding of language in use. We now have access to simple and unobtrusive audio and video recording technology, and we can make use of sophisticated approaches to the transcription and analysis of interactional data. With these resources available, there is no reason why descriptive linguistics cannot develop into a more strongly data-based field of knowledge.

Notes

1 Introduction

1 CA has been criticized for being heavily English-based (but see Moerman 1977). This is not, however, a drawback with respect to the present study, as my database is strictly English. Clearly, much CA work remains to be done using data from languages other than English.
2 This pressure is particularly felt in conversations with three or more participants, in which the determination of next speakership is problematic.
3 See Sacks *et al.* (1974), pp. 720–723, for other suggestions on the interaction between grammar and the turn-taking system.
4 This case is analyzed in chapter 3, section 3.3.2.
5 In a complete CA account, this interpretation would be supported or refuted by the participant talk that follows the particular sequence.

2 Overview of the conversational corpus

1 Because there are alternative methods of transcription even within the CA tradition, I have retranscribed sections of some of the original transcripts in order to keep the conventions consistent throughout my presentation.

3 Initial adverbial clauses

1 This leads to a more detailed discussion of interactional contexts than other approaches to conversation might demand.
2 See Hinrichs (1986) and Smith (1980) for discussions of temporal anaphora in discourse.
3 See Jefferson (1978) for a discussion of story beginnings.
4 See Jefferson (1973):57–71 for an examination of the interactional import of such early placement of responses.
5 This data is analyzed in Schegloff 1987.

6 For discussions of the interactional significance of pauses see Pomerantz (1978, 1984) and Davidson (1984).
7 This *since*-clause and the partial *since*-clause in V's response are the only cases of potentially initial causal clauses in the data. C's *since*-clause is the only complete causal clause, but as it functions without a main clause, it cannot strictly be classified as an initial adverbial clause. These cases are discussed in chapter 6.
8 The V in this example is a different person than V in example 18.
9 The *if*-clause in this example is not an embedded question. In fact, it is the embedded question that is interrupted for the insertion of the *if*.
10 In their cross-linguistic research on politeness, Brown and Levinson (1987) note that interlocutors avoid expressing assumptions regarding a hearer's wants. This leads to hedging in environments where one speaker could be imposing on a recipient (pp. 146–147). Brown and Levinson also point to adverbial clauses as vehicles for such hedges (pp. 162–164).
11 Managing turn taking must be done in combination with structuring information. This can result in initial, rather than final, placement where discourse shift work is especially appropriate, as in the exposition of contrasting options or of longer sequences of events. See chapter 4 (4.3.3) for a discussion of the general distribution of initial adverbial clauses in relation to the turn-taking system.
12 The previous two categories of initial adverbial clause functions, managing time frames and stating options, each consisted of one clause type, temporals and conditionals, respectively. But, while the contrast category is comprised primarily of conditional clauses (n = 10), it also contains one temporal, one concessive, and one causal.

4 Final versus initial adverbial clauses in continuous intonation

1 Concessives are ignored here for the sake of simplicity. Adverbial clauses without main clauses are not included in this table.
2 Examples 17 and 19 in chapter 3 involved repair associated with initial conditional clauses. However, there the repair was not of already-in-progress adverbial clauses. Those cases contained repairs involving the insertion of adverbial clauses.
3 For other approaches to the turn-taking system see Duncan and Fiske (1977) and a general review by Wilson, Wiemann, and Zimmerman (1984).
4 In this and other frequency tables that follow, I am considering the adverbial clause, not the individual speaking, to be the unit of observation. As mentioned earlier, there were 33 different speakers in the database. A larger database, and a more powerful statistical tool than chi-square, would be needed to factor out the influence of individuals on patterns of adverbial clause usage. See Hatch and Lazaraton (1991) for a discussion of the use of the chi-square statistic on text data.

5 The average lengths for temporals and conditionals remain constant even when initial or finally placed clauses are counted separately. The differences displayed in Table 9 are not biased by the fact that both initial and final temporals and conditionals are included.

6 There is no particular warrant for using words as a metric; they simply provide a convenient and accessible way of measuring relative length. For these counts, words transcribed as units were treated as single words; so *gonna* and *that's* were each counted as one word. This was done for all clause types so it is not likely to have biased the counts in either direction. An upper limit of clause length was set at 20 words, and, in fact, several causal clauses went over that limit but were counted as containing 20 words.

7 I thank Manny Schegloff for drawing this point to my attention.

5 Final adverbial clauses after ending intonation

1 The fact that other speakers have the opportunity to come in at these locations is attested to by the statistical significance in the length of the gap for the onset of same speaker as compared with other speaker talk, the latter being shorter (Sacks, Schegloff and Jefferson 1974:54 n 30). Also, see Wilson and Zimmerman (1986) for a study supporting the Sacks *et al.* observations regarding the operation of the turn-taking system. Ford and Thompson (to appear) examines the relationships between grammar, intonation, semantics, and speaker change.

2 Abraham (1991) looks at the alternation between *because* and *because of* in spoken and written English, relating their distribution to a given/new distinction involving more than simply noun phrases.

3 For discussions of adverbial clauses which modify speech acts, see Rutherford (1970) and Brown and Yule (1983:227–228).

4 There was one PCE that did not fit neatly into any of the above categories. This was a temporal that appears after final intonation, apparently because the speaker had trouble in the middle of what would have probably been an intonationally coherent unit. This case is discussed in section 6.4 of the next chapter.

```
C: Keegan used to race uhr uh- er it was um, (0.4) used to run
   um (2.7) Oh:: shit.
   (0.4)
C: Uhm,
   (0.4)
C: Fisher's car.
M: Three an'⎡a  ⎡quarter
P:          ⎣   ⎣Need some more i⎡ce.
C:              ⎣Three an' an quarter.   ⎣
M:                                       ⎣Yeh.
   (1.0)
C: When I was foolin' around.                        (AD 17.19)
```

5 See Lerner 1987 for a full discussion of collaboration in conversation.
6 In interpreting N's *too*, we must assume that N has inferred some other motivation for H's offering to drive, and it is to that first motivation that this second one (N's closeness to the destination) is added.
7 For further discussion of the co-telling in this conversation, see Schegloff 1988.

6 Comparison of clause types and apparent deviations from the general patterns

1 Sweetser (1990:123–132) presents an insightful discussion of the semantics of conditionals and of Haiman's association of conditionals with topics. Sweetser refers to the way certain conditionals "may show how the speech act fits into the structure of the jointly constructed conversational world" (p. 131).
2 See Schiffrin (1987) for a discussion of *because* in this pattern as a discourse marker.
3 Recognition of the contingency of this kind of plan proposal is felicity condition on such speech acts in the analysis of Brown and Levinson (1987).
4 Marianne Celce-Murcia has brought to my attention that it is significant that *since* rather than *because* or *'cause* should be used initially. *Since* is associated with a summing up function and is potentially interpretable as "given that." *Since*, then, has a slightly different meaning than *because* or *cause*.

7 Conclusion

1 See Ford (1992) for further discussion of the separation of adverbial clauses from main clauses in speech and writing.

References

Abraham, Elyse. 1991. Why "because"? The management of given/new information as a constraint on the selection of causal alternatives. *Text*, 11–3: 323–339.
Atkinson, J. Maxwell. 1984. Public speaking and audience responses: some techniques for inviting applause. In *Structures of social action*, ed. by J. Maxwell Atkinson and John Heritage. Cambridge University Press.
Atkinson, J. Maxwell and P. Drew. 1979. *Order in the court.* London: Macmillan.
Atkinson, J. Maxwell and John Heritage eds. 1984. *Structures of social action.* Cambridge University Press.
Beaman, Karen. 1984. Coordination and subordination revisited: Syntactic complexity in spoken and written narrative discourse. In *Coherence in spoken and written discourse*, ed. by Deborah Tannen. Norwood, NJ: Ablex.
Biber, Douglas, 1986. Spoken and written textual dimensions in English: Resolving the contradictory findings. *Language*, 62: 384–416.
Brown, Gillian and George Yule. 1983. *Discourse analysis.* Cambridge University Press.
Brown, Penelope and Stephen C. Levinson. 1987. *Politeness: Some universals in language usage.* Cambridge University Press.
Button, Graham and Neil Casey. 1984. Generating topic: the use of topic initial elicitors. In *Structures of social action*, ed. by J. Maxwell Atkinson and John Heritage. Cambridge University Press.
Celce-Murcia, Marianne, and Diane Larsen-Freeman. 1983. *The grammar book: and ESL/EFL teacher's course.* Rowley, MA: Newbury House.
Chafe, Wallace L. 1984. How people use adverbial clauses. In *The proceedings of the tenth annual meeting of the Berkeley Linguistics Society.* Berkeley Lingusitics Society.
   1987. *Cognitive constraints on information flow. Coherence and grounding in discourse*, ed. by Russell Tomlin. Amsterdam: Benjamins.

Chafe, Wallace L. 1988. Linking intonation units in spoken English. In *Clause combining in grammar and discourse*, ed. by John Haiman and Sandra A. Thompson. Amsterdam: Benjamins.

Chafe, Wallace L. and Jane Danielewicz. 1985. *Properties of spoken and written language. Comprehending oral and written language*, ed. by Rosalind Horowitz and S. J. Samuels. New York: Academic Press.

Daneš, F. 1974. Functional sentence perspective and the organization of the text. In *Papers on functional sentence perspective*, ed. by F. Daneš. Prague: Academia.

Davidson, Judy. 1984. Subsequent versions of invitations, offers, requests, and proposals dealing with potential or actual rejection. In *Structures of social action*, ed. by J. Maxwell Atkinson and John Heritage. Cambridge University Press.

Douglas, Carol Anne. 1987. Charlotte Bunch on global feminism. *Off Our Backs*, 17–9: 10–12.

Du Bois, John W. 1984. Competing motivations. In *Iconicity in syntax*, ed. by John Haiman. Amsterdam: Benjamins.

Duncan, S. and D. W. Fiske. 1977. *Face-to-face interaction*. Hillsdale, NJ: Erlbaum.

Ford, Cecilia E. 1987. Overlapping relations in text structure. In *The proceedings of the second annual meeting of the Pacific linguistics conference*, ed. by Scott DeLancey and Russell Tomlin. University of Oregon.

1992. Variation in the intonation and punctuation of different adverbial clause types in spoken and written English. In *The linguistics of literacy*, ed. by P. Downing, S. Lima, and M. Noonan. Amsterdam: Benjamins.

Ford, Cecilia E. and Sandra A. Thompson. 1986. Conditionals in discourse: a text-based study from English. In *On conditionals*, ed. by E. Traugott, C. Ferguson, J. Snitzer Reilly, and A. ter Meulen. Cambridge: University Press.

Unpublished. *Projectability in conversation: Grammar, intonation, and semantics*.

Fries, Peter. 1983. On the status of theme in English: arguments from discourse. In *Micro and macro connexity of texts*, ed. by J. S. Petofi and Emel Sozer. Hamburg: Helmut Buske Verlag.

Givón, Talmy. 1984. *Syntax: A functional typological introduction*, I. Amsterdam: Benjamins.

Goffman, Erving. 1967. *Interaction ritual: Essays on face-to-face behavior*. New York: Anchor.

Haiman, John. 1978. Conditionals are topics. *Language*, 54: 564–589.

Halliday, M. A. K. 1967. Notes on transitivity and theme in English: Part 2. *Journal of Linguistics* 3: 199–244.

1970. *A course in spoken English: intonation*. Oxford: University Press.

1973. *Explorations in the functions of language*. London: Edward Arnold.

References

Hatch, Evelyn M. and Ann Lazaraton. 1991. *The research manual: design and statistics for applied linguistics.* Boston: Newbury House.

Heritage, John. 1984. *Garfinkel and ethnomethodology.* Cambridge: Polity Press.

Hinrichs, Erhard. 1986. Temporal anaphora in discourses of English. *Linguistics and Philosophy*, 9: 63–82.

Jefferson, Gail. 1973. A case of precision timing in ordinary conversation: overlapped tag-positioned address terms in closing sequences. *Semiotica*, 9: 47–96.

  1974. Error correction as an interactional resource. *Language in Society*, 2: 181–199.

  1978. Sequential aspects of storytelling in conversation. *Studies in the organization of conversational interaction*, ed. by Jim Schenkein. New York: Academic Press.

  1981. "Caveat speaker": a preliminary exploration of shift implicative recipiency in the articulation of topic. End of Grant Report. London: Social Science Research Council. Mimeo.

Leech, Geoffrey and Jan Svartvik. 1975. *A communicative grammar of English.* London: Longman.

Lerner, G. H. 1987. Collaborative turn sequences: sentence construction and social action. Unpublished dissertation. University of California, Irvine.

Levinson, Stephen C. 1983. *Pragmatics.* Cambridge University Press.

Linde, Charlotte. 1976. Constraints on the ordering of *if*-clauses. In *The proceedings of the second annual meeting of the Berkeley Linguistics Society*. Berkeley Linguistics Society.

Linde, Charlotte and William Labov. 1975. Spatial networks as a site for the study of language and thought. *Language*, 51: 924–939.

Longacre, Robert, and Sandra A. Thompson. 1985. Adverbial clauses. *Language typology and syntactic description*, ed. by Timothy Shopen. Cambridge University Press.

Mathesius, V. 1942. From comparative word order studies. *Casopis pro Moderni Filoligii*, 28.

Matthiessen, Christian, and Sandra A. Thompson. 1988. The structure of discourse and "subordination." *Clause combining in discourse and grammar*, ed. by John Haiman and Sandra A. Thompson. Amsterdam: Benjamins.

Moerman, M. 1977. The preference for self-correction in a Tai conversational corpus. *Language*, 53–4: 872–882.

Orestrom, Bengt. 1983. *Turn-taking in English conversation. Lund studies in English.* Lund: Gleerup.

Pomerantz, A. 1978. Compliment responses: notes on the co-operation of multiple constraints. In *Studies in the organization of conversational interaction*, ed. by Jim Schenkein, New York: Academic Press.

  1984. Pursuing a response. In *Structures of social action*, ed. by J. Maxwell Atkinson and John Heritage. Cambridge University Press.

Quirk, Randolf and Sidney Greenbaum. 1973. *A concise grammar of contemporary English*. New York: Harcourt Brace Jovanovich.
Quirk, Randolf, Sidney Greenbaum, Geoffrey Leech, and Jan Svartvik. 1985. *A comprehensive grammar of the English language*. London: Longman.
Ramsay, Violeta. 1987. The functional distribution of preposed and postposed "if" and "when" clauses in written narrative. In *Coherence and grounding in discourse*, ed. by R. S. Tomlin. Amsterdam: Benjamins.
Rutherford, W. 1970. Some observation concerning subordinate clauses. *Language*, 46: 97–115.
Sacks, Harvey. 1972. On the analyzability of stories by children. In *Directions in sociolinguistics*, ed. by John J. Gumperz and Dell H. Hymes. New York: Holt, Rinehart and Winston.
  1974. An analysis of the course of a joke's telling in conversation. In *Explorations in the ethnography of speaking*, ed. by R. Bauman and J. Sherzer. Cambridge University Press.
  1987. On the preferences for agreement and contiguity in sequences in conversation. In *Talk and social organisation*, ed. by Graham Button and John R. E. Lee. Philadelphia: Multilingual Matters.
Sacks, Harvey, Emanuel A. Schegloff, and Gail Jefferson. 1974. A simplest systematics for the organization of turn-taking for conversation. *Language*, 50: 696–735.
Schegloff, Emanuel A. 1968. Sequencing in conversational openings. *American Anthropologist*, 70: 1075–1095.
  1972. Notes on conversational practice: formulating place. In *Studies in social interaction*, ed. by David Sudnow. New York: Free Press.
  1976. On some questions and ambiguities in conversation. Pragmatics microfiche 2.2: D8–G1 (reprinted in Atkinson and Heritage 1984).
  1980. Preliminaries to preliminaries: "Can I ask you a question?" *Sociological Inquiry*, ed. by D. Zimmerman and C. West, 50: 104–152.
  1987. Discourse as an interactional achievement II: an exercise in conversation analysis. In *Linguistics in context: connecting observation and understanding*, ed. by Deborah Tannen. Norwood, NJ: Ablex.
  1988. Description in the social sciences I: Talk in interaction. *Papers in Pragmatics*, 2-1/2: 1–24.
Schegloff, Emanuel A. and Harvey Sacks. 1973. Opening up closings. *Semiotica* 7: 289–327.
Schegloff, Emanuel A., Gail Jefferson and Harvey Sacks. 1977. The preference for self-correction in the organization of repair in conversation. *Language*, 53: 361–382.
Schiffrin, Deborah. 1985. Multiple constraints on discourse options: a quantitative analysis of causal sequences. *Discourse Processes*, 8: 281–303.

1987. *Discourse markers*. Cambridge University Press.
Silva, Marilyn N. 1981. Perception and the choice of language in oral narrative: the case of the co-temporal connectives. In *The proceedings of the seventh annual meeting of the Berkeley Linguistics Society*. Berkeley Linguistics Society. 284–294.
Smith, Carlota. 1980. Temporal structures in discourse. In *Time, tense and quantifiers, proceedings of the Stuttgart conference on the logic of tense and quantification*. Niemeyer, Tübingen, 335–374.
Sweetser, Eve E. 1990. *From etymology to pragmatics: Metaphorical and cultural aspects of semantic structure*. Cambridge University Press.
Taylor, Talbot J. and Deborah Cameron. 1987. *Analysing conversation: Rules and units in the structure of talk*. Oxford: Pergamon Press.
Thompson, Sandra A. 1985a. "Subordination" in formal and informal discourse. In *Meaning, form and use in Context, Proceedings of the 1984 Georgetown University Roundtable on Linguistics*, ed. by Deborah Schiffrin. Washington, DC, Georgetown: University Press.
  1985b. Grammar and written discourse: initial vs. final purpose clauses in English. *Text*, 5: 55–84.
  1987. "Subordination" and narrative event structure. In *Coherence and grounding in discourse*, ed. by Russell S. Tomlin. Amsterdam: Benjamins.
van Dijk, Teun A. 1977. *Text and context*. London: Longman.
Wilson, T. P., J. Weiman, and D. H. Zimmerman. 1984. Models of turn taking in conversational interaction. *Journal of Language and Social Psychology*, 3-3: 159–183.
Wilson, T. P. and D. H. Zimmerman. 1986. The structure of silence between turns in two-party conversation. *Discourse Processes*, 9: 375–390.

Author index

Abraham, E., 153n
Atkinson, J. M., 107, 119

Beaman, K., 19
Biber, D., 19, 149
Brown, G., 65, 153n
Brown, P., 2, 15, 152n, 154n
Bunch, C., 86
Button, G., 9

Cameron, D., 2
Casey, N., 9
Celce-Murcia, M., 138, 149, 154n
Chafe, W. L., 11, 17, 68, 102–103, 123

Daneš, F., 65
Davidson, J., 117, 119, 152n
Douglas, C. A., 86
Drew, P., 107, 119
Du Bois, J. W., 1
Duncan, S., 152n

Fiske, D. W., 152n
Ford, C. E., 4, 11, 14–15, 42, 47, 59, 68, 133, 153–154n
Fries, P., 12, 65

Givón, T., 76
Goffman, E., 2
Greenbaum, S., 138

Haiman, J., 14, 132–133, 154n
Halliday, M. A. K., 65
Hatch, E. M., 152n
Heritage, J., 2
Hinrichs, E., 151n

Jefferson, G., 2–11, 78–81, 104, 111, 151n, 153n

Labov, W., 12
Larsen-Freeman, D., 138, 149
Lazaraton, A., 152n
Leech, G., 138
Lerner, G. H., 154n
Levinson, S. C., 2, 6–10, 15, 107, 119, 152n, 154n
Linde, C., 11–12, 15
Longacre, R., 104

Mathesius, V., 65
Matthiessen, C., 104
Moerman, M., 151n

Orestrom, B., 4

Pomerantz, A., 108, 152n

Quirk, R., 138

Ramsay, V., 11, 15–16, 32, 68
Rutherford, W., 153n

Sacks, H., 2–11, 47, 57, 78–81, 104, 106, 111, 151n, 153n
Schegloff, E. A., 2–11, 47, 78–81, 104, 111, 151n, 153–154n
Schiffrin, D., 11, 16–18, 63, 85, 88, 106, 154n
Silva, M. N., 11, 16
Smith, C., 151n
Svartvik, J., 138
Sweetser, E. E., 15, 154n

Taylor, T. J., 2
Thompson, S. A., 4, 11–15, 18–19, 32, 42, 47, 59, 68, 104, 133–134, 153

Wiemann, J., 152n
Wilson, T. P., 119, 152–153n

Yule, G., 65, 153n

Zimmerman, D. H., 119, 152–153n

Subject index

accounts, 9, 50, 107, 114–116, 143–144
adjacency pairs, 7–10
　expansion, 9
　insertion, 9
adverbial clauses
　bidirectionality, 11
　cognitive complexity, 86–93, 142–144, 147
　comparison between types, 130–136, 144–145
　deviation from general patterns, 139–144
　following final intonation, *see* post-completion extensions
　frequency of types, 24–25
　guiding function, 12
　information flow, 17–18
　initial vs. final, 11–18, 63–90; turn taking, and, 78–85
　intonation, 17, 21, 24–25, 27, 90–91, 135–136
　length, 88–90
　overview of types in database, 23–25
　placement of types, 24
　prior studies, 11–20
　requirements for, 23
　speech and writing, 18–20
afterthoughts, 17–18, 102–103, 123, 130; *see also* post-completion extensions
already, 70
anticipatory linkage, 89–90, 100

because-clauses, 16–17, 85–100, 125–129
　distinct characteristics of, 85–93
　evaluation, after, 96–98, 99–100
　interactional emergence of, 93, 102–130
　interview data, in, 86–87
　intonation, 90–91
　jointly asserted with main clauses, 98–100
　pauses and disfluencies, 91–93
　planned discourse, 86–87
　presupposed information, 94–96, 99–100
before, 34–37, 126
bidirectionality, 11
by the time, 71

cataphora, 93–96
causal clauses; *see also because*-clauses
　planning constraints, 86–93, 142–144
chi-square statistic, 152n
collaboration, 154n; *see under* post-completion extensions
commands, *see under* post-completion extensions
conditional relevance, 9–10
conditionals, *see also if*-clauses
　semantics, 154n; *see also if*-clauses
　topics, as, 132–133
continuers, 30, 82; *see also* extended turns, recipient contributions
contrast
　main clauses, 75–78
　if-clauses, 15, 53–54, 56–61
conversation analysis, 2–11
　English-based, 151n
　other models, 2, 152n
conversation vs. monologue, 78
corpus, *see* database

database, 21–25
　limitations of, 21–23
　participants in, 21–23

163

delicate talk, 44–47, 56
disagreement, 8; *see also* dispreferred, preference, preferred responses
discourse marker, 154n
disfluencies, 52, 71; *see also under because*-clauses, pauses
dispreferred responses, 8–9, 106–124

early placement of responses, 36, 151n
every time, 34–37
extended turns, 4–5, 29–31, 79–85
   recipient contributions to, 30–37, 82

failing topic, 36
final adverbial clauses
   after ending intonation, *see* post-completion extensions
   afterthoughts, 17–18, 102, 123, 130
   alternating with prepositional phrases, 71–73
   conditional, 74–78
   intonation, 63–64
   local semantic function, 14, 134
   repair, 71–72
   temporal, 67–73
   turn taking, 78–85
first pair part, 7–10, 107
first starter rights, 5

hedging, 15, 152n
hesitations, 9, 44, 50, 71; *see also* pauses
hypotheticality, 15, 44–47, 146

if-clauses, 14–16, 57–61, 74–78, 84, 127, 132–134, 152n
   creating temporary discourse realities, 133
   hypotheticality, 15, 44–47, 146
   without main clauses, 136–139
initial adverbial clauses, 26–62
   contrasting, 15, 56–61
   discourse connection and, 65–67
   discourse role, 134
   information patterns, 26–62
   interactional functions, 26–62
   intonation, 27
   scope, 30
   shift function, 26, 28–42, *see also* adverbial clauses, guiding function
   theme, 65–67
   without main clauses, 27, 45, 47, 49–50
initial *if*-clauses, 42–56
   assuming information, 47
   delicate talk, 44–47, 56

displaying interpretation of prior talk, 43
   options, 42–56
   persuasion, 47–50, 56
   problematic contingencies, 44
   projecting contrast, 53–54
   reported speech, 51–56
   shared information, 50–51
interpretation
   participants as sources, 3, 6–7, 27, 151n
   sequence and, 2, 9–10, 27
intonation, 17, 21, 24–25, 27, 90–91, 135–136; *see also under because*-clauses, final adverbial clauses, initial adverbial clauses, turn-taking

monitor spaces, 119

negation, 76–78
next turn repair initiators (NTRI), 111–113
non-anticipatory linkage, 87, 90

pauses, 9, 31, 36, 38, 45–46, 91–93, 108–112, 123, 141, 152n
persuasion, 47–50, 56
post-completion extensions (PCEs), 102–130, 135
   accounts as, 114–116
   afterthoughts, 102–103, 123, 130
   background, 120–121
   collaboration, 124–129; displaying agreement, 124–126; checking understanding, 126–127; co-telling, 127–129
   different speakers, 124–129
   explanatory, 119–120
   information packaging, 119
   minimal responses after, 110
   pauses, 108–112, 123
   preference, 106–124
   prompted, 107–117, 122–123
   pursuing responses, 107–111, 117–119
   questions and commands, 117–120
   same speakers, 104–124
   self-editing, 119–124
   speaker-recipient negotiation, 102–130
pre-closing, 47–50
pre-evaluation, 96–97
preference, 7–10, 57–58, 61; *see also under* post-completion extensions
   orienting toward, 8, 57–58, 61

Subject index

primary speakership, 80–85, 105
projectability, *see* turn projection *under* turn-taking
purpose clauses, 13–14
pursuing responses, *see under* post-completion extensions

qualitative vs. quantitative analysis, 19
quantification, 16, 18–20, 152n
questions, *see under* post-completion extensions

repair, 54, 71–72, 152n; *see also* next turn repair initiators; recipient contributions *under* extended turns
reported speech, 51–56

second pair part, 7–10, 107; relevance of, 7
semantically broad terms, 29–33, 41–42
sequential context, 7–11
shaping, *see* preference, orienting toward
since, 23, 59, 70, 142–144, 152n
vs. *because*, 154n
so, 87–90, 100
speaker–recipient negotiation, *see under* post-completion extensions
speech act theory, 2, 154n

temporal anaphora, 151n
theme, 12, 65–67
then, 32–33, 41–42; *see also* semantically broad terms
thing, 29–30, 41–42; *see also* semantically broad terms
though, 114
time frames
introducing, 28–31
shifting, 28, 31–42
toning down, 38
transcription, 21, 151n
conventions, xii–xiii
intonation, of, 21
transcripts, key to, 22–23
transition relevance places, *see under* turn taking
turn constructional units, *see under* turn taking
turn taking, 3–6
clause placement and, 78–85
completion points, 4–6; avoidance of, 4, 51–56
grammar, 5–6, 78–85, 151n
intonation, 4, 103–105
other models, 2, 152n
post-completion extensions, 104–106
speaker and recipient work, 4–5, 30–37, 82
transition relevance places, 5–6
turn extension, 5–6, 29–32
turn projection, 3–6, 29–32; pragmatic, 81
turn-constructional units, 5–6, 104

well, 8, 107–108
when-clauses, 16, 28–33, 37–42, 56, 66–73, 137, 140–141
whenever, 37–38
word searches, 30; *see also* extended turns, recipient contributions